The Agile PMO
SUCCEEDING WITH AGILE GOVERNANCE

BY PAUL OSBORN

PAUL osborn

SUCCEEDING WITH AGILE GOVERNANCE

← the Agile PMO

some KEY principles

"planning is everything,
PERPETUAL PLANNING
plans are nothing"

cadence

★ Make **BIG** decisions *infrequently*

★ Make SMALL decisions *frequently*

An AGILE PMO

→ protects autonomy of agile team

→ defends the agile process across disciplines

→ helps provides logistical support...think reporting & procurement

Yo...check this out...

AGILE WILL RESULT IN GREATER PROBLEMS VS FEWER PROBLEMS IF NOT PRACTICED OUTSIDE OF TECH

Preface

About "The Agile PMO" Series

I wrote the "The Agile PMO" series of books to help you and your program manager understand exactly where the Program Management Office (PMO) fits into the new Agile world order. Armed with this knowledge you will be equipped to ensure that the whole organization is "succeeding with Agile". I am not intending for this series to be an introduction to Agile, and so if that is what you are looking for, you may safely put this back on the shelf. Instead it is intended for managers and executives in organizations that have been employing Agile but would like to get more benefit from it. You probably already have several teams working in Scrum, the most popular method in the United States, or are using another Agile methodology. "The Agile PMO" books are intended for organizations like yours. I won't spend a lot of time talking about the mechanics of stories, story points, iterations, showcases and retrospectives. If you want to know about those things then there are some excellent books out there – Mike Cohn has a fantastic series of books that I highly recommend – so this book is neither a Scrum nor an Agile primer.

However, if you have been doing Agile for a while you may be having frequent run-ins with your executive team about annual budgeting, what the team is working on now, whether the team is working hard enough, and what the status of the project is. You may have come across conflicts between the teams and Product Management about how the solution has been defined, why they can't commit to the date the product manager agreed with the client to, what constitutes an adequate solution, and, oh yes, whether the team is working hard enough. If so, you might need help from an Agile PMO.

What is an Agile PMO?

If you think that an Agile PMO is an oxymoron, then I wrote this book *especially for you*. Indeed, why are we talking about the Program Management Office (PMO) in a world of self-organized teams, decentralized control, and light project management methods? PMOs are associated with the heavy project management requirements of Waterfall development, where rigor and adherence to defined processes created a need for a centralized office of project management. Considering that the three functions of a PMO are to (1) manage project managers, (2) define and govern processes, and (3) be responsible for executing strategic programs, aren't these largely unnecessary in an Agile software organization?

An *Agile* PMO however, is more than just a PMO that operates within an Agile software development organization. An *Agile* PMO has distinct roles within, and around, the Agile process. It defends and protects the autonomy of the Agile teams, helps or substitutes for, scrum masters and scrum coaches, defends the Agile process, defines how cross-functional processes interact with the Agile process, provides quality control for the approval and governance process, and provides logistical support such as management reporting and tool procurement for the project teams. Because I am concerned with the role rather than the job title, I don't distinguish between an organization with a specialized PMO department, just one person with that title, or employees who perform the role as part of another job function.

The particular challenges of an Agile PMO, compared to a PMO operating in a more 'traditional' environment, are rooted in the Agile Manifesto (Beck, et al., 2001). The full Manifesto is reprinted in the Appendix for your reference. A traditional PMO is mostly about the right-hand side of the Agile Manifesto – the side that is commonly associated with Waterfall. On the right, there are activities such as instigating and monitoring processes, ensuring comprehensive documentation, negotiating contracts, and ensuring that the plan is followed. Unfortunately not even an Agile PMO can get away with not doing some or all of these activities to some extent or other, and so it is important to remind ourselves that the Manifesto is a spectrum, not a dichotomy, and that when used appropriately right-hand side activities still do have value… *"That is, while **there is value in the items on the right**, we value the items on the left more"* (emphasis added). Even though documentation and plans are more prevalent in the PMO than in Agile software development teams, that doesn't **necessarily** mean that the PMO practices aren't 'Agile'.

Extract from the Agile Manifesto

The Items on the Left…	The Items on the Right…
Individuals And Interactions	Processes And Tools
Working Software	Comprehensive Documentation
Customer Collaboration	Contract Negotiation
Responding To Change	Following A Plan

PROGLEMS
of governance

Defining the solution too early

* project requirements can be more & more entrenched
* initial assumptions become less valid...
  ...YET MORE DEFENDED
* a sub-optimal product *will* be built. Sux, ha.

Making too many decisions

☆ never enough time to finish a feature
☆ always a fire to put out
☆ team working on too many initiatives at a time

DO LESS. COMPLETE MORE.
Throughput over max utilization, silly.

Detailed project plans

☆ too much upfront planning...when **details are unknown**
☆ too many plans...creating **conflicts**
☆ too document centric... too **rigid**

Executives view AGILE as something tech does

| *AGILE requires support across* ▶ | **VALUE STREAMS** *and* across **MANAGERS** |

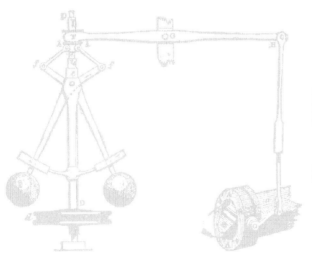

I.
Problems of Governance

The Role of Governance

When I look at any successful governance framework, I look for three key elements – processes, artifacts, and people. Specifically I look for:

1. **Processes and structures to approve or deny projects**. It's pretty common to see pre-defined approval gates to approve or deny projects. Often tailored to the size of the project being approved, approval gates are designed to sequentially filter out projects until only the most valuable are left.

2. **The apparatus to effectively collect, communicate, and preserve information**. Almost every successful organization has standardized templates for business cases, requirement documents, and project plans.

3. **A framework for defining roles and responsibilities**. Determining who decides what, and who does what, is commonly portrayed through an accountability matrix which delegates responsibility, power, and authority to participants.

If all three elements are present and functioning properly, the chances are that the organization has a controlled, auditable decision-making process. We should see that the product development value stream is effectively and efficiently turning market strategies into working software. From this we see that the role of governance is in:

- Providing auditable decision-making.
- Controlling the value stream.

PROVIDING AUDITABLE DECISION MAKING

Software development is both expensive and important, and therefore we need to be able to provide regulatory and management oversight for it. We achieve that oversight through governance. Accounting standards from the US GAAP or IFRS need to be satisfied when software is capitalized. We need to demonstrate that the software will both be profitable, and capable of surviving the three or five years that the project is being capitalized over. How do we do that? We do it through business cases, requirement documents, and other tangible evidence of customer and executive involvement.

Even if we aren't capitalizing development costs, we will still need to satisfy the Board and shareholders that their money is being responsibly spent. In good times top-line sales figures are probably enough, but in all other times a solid governance process for documenting and justifying decisions goes a long way.

CONTROLLING THE VALUE STREAM

I have found that a typical software development organization has two primary value streams:

1. The sales and customer service value stream.
2. The product development value stream.

There are many more processes and departments involved in creating software than just the product owner and development teams. How do we manage this complexity? We achieve this through governance. Controlling myriad processes and departments to make the best use of valuable resources takes effort and discipline, and it is governance that provides a framework for making decisions throughout the value stream.

What are Value Streams?

"Value stream" is a term from Lean that describes a full end-to-end production process. Typically, the input to the value stream is a request for some product by a customer, and the output is the delivery of that product to the customer. For example, Toyota has a manufacturing value stream that builds a car once you order one from one of their showrooms.

Value streams are comprised of two basic elements – processes and queues. The 'work product', such as a car, moves through the value stream going from one process to the next. The product starts 'upstream' and moves 'downstream' until completion. When the work product is between processes, it is put in a queue. These queues are often referred to as 'inventory stores' and they represent partially finished product, and are a therefore a large constituent of Work-in-Progress (WIP).

Processes take work product from the inventory store that is immediately upstream, do some type of transformation on the product, and then place it in the inventory store immediately downstream to them.

The Sales & Customer Service Value Stream

I like to refer to the sales and customer service value stream by its value proposition of 'creating happy customers'. The inputs to this value stream are "unhappy people with problems". The outputs are "happy, productive evangelists". It is the job of your marketing communications people, along with the product marketers, to position the product to potential buyers. It is the job of the sales team to sell them the product. Depending on how complex the product is, customer service personnel might install the software and train the users. Product marketers enter the stream again at the end to evaluate how the product is being received in the market. The results of the feedback from marketing will either be incorporated into the product positioning of the customer service value stream, or into the product development value stream as a newly identified market problem.

The Sales & Customer Service Value Stream

MARKET POSITIONING	SALES COLLATERAL	PROSPECT IDENTIFICATION	SALES PIPELINE MANAGEMENT
· PRODUCT MARKETING	· SALES · PRODUCT MARKETING	· SALES	· SALES

TRAINING AND SUPPORT	RENEWALS	OPERATIONAL SUPPORT	WIN/LOSS ANALYSIS
· TRAINING · CUSTOMER SUPPORT	· CUSTOMER SUPPORT · RENEWAL SALES	· SOFTWARE DEVELOPMENT	· PRODUCT MARKETING

The sales and customer service value stream has a cycle time which roughly corresponds to the sales cycle and so is often less than one year long.

The Product Development Value Stream

I like to refer to the product development value stream by its value proposition of 'solving market problems'. Its inputs are market problems, and its outputs are software solutions. It starts with marketers identifying suitable market problems. From those problems a market strategy is formulated. Often the market strategy will be planned and funded during an annual budgeting process. Over the course of the following year, the software is designed and developed by solution delivery teams comprising of user researchers, interaction designers, developers, and test engineers. The software is then brought to market – either in a shrink-wrapped CD, or as is more common nowadays, as a service hosted somewhere in the cloud.

The Product Development Value Stream

IDENTIFY NEW MARKET PROBLEMS	IDENTIFY NEW MARKET SEGMENTS	3-5 YEAR STRATEGY	ANNUAL PLANNING
· PRODUCT MARKETING	· PRODUCT MARKETING	· EXECUTIVE STEERING	· PRODUCT MANAGEMENT · EXECUTIVE STEERING

PRODUCT SOLUTIONING	CODING	TESTING	INTERNAL TRAINING
· ARCHITECTS · INTERACTION DESIGNERS	· SOFTWARE DEVELOPMENT	· SOFTWARE DEVELOPMENT	· TRAINING

INSTALL/ MAINTAIN PHYSICAL PROD ENVIRONMENT	DEPLOY SOFTWARE TO PRODUCTION	CONTROL MONITOR APP USAGE & PERMORMANCE
· IT INFRASTRUCTURE	· DEV OPS	· DEV OPS

The product development value stream has cycle times that typically span many years, and consumes millions of dollars. Agile software development is just one part - albeit an important part - of this value stream, and helping all these parts fit together to form a cohesive whole is the role of the governance process.

Governance In
An Agile Organization

Agile methodologies operate within only a small part of the whole product development value stream. Agile methodologies are addressing the problem of forever changing and unknowable requirements that is being created upstream in the Product Marketing and Product Management departments.

If Agile is implemented only in the Technology department, while the Product Marketing and Management departments do not change their own processes, it can result in greater, not fewer problems. When partially or mechanically implemented in this way Agile becomes an *enabler*, allowing the product managers to escape the consequences of poor decisions and sloppy thinking. ***If Agile embraces and welcomes change, then change is what Product Management will give it.*** If at the same time governance is reduced or even eliminated as being "anti-Agile", there will be no plan by which anyone is held accountable. Chaos is encouraged, and indeed chaos will ensue.

The need to respond to change decisively makes governance even more important in an Agile environment than a slower responding, more traditional one. Whether or not you have a formal program management function, if you choose to use an Agile software process then some form of Agile governance will be necessary. Trying to use existing, non-Agile, governance policies will inevitably create crippling conflict.

We can certainly create our own Agile governance process, or we can leverage existing governance frameworks that exist with Stage-Gate®, Pragmatic Marketing®, DSDM Atern®, or the Balanced Scorecard® among others. In a medium sized company with less than 10 or 20 major value stream stakeholders, tailoring the governance process is often the wisest option because adopting a large framework of this nature is extremely difficult – touching as it does the entire value stream and reaching deep up into the office of the Chief Executive. Indeed, I have found that most small- or medium-sized organizations, and even a surprisingly large number of big organizations, have ad-hoc processes and that these are often built around the Chief Executive's personality, or even the **previous** Chief Executive's personality!

However, should you be in the fortunate position of being able to start from scratch or if one of the standard frameworks is already in place, then standard frameworks are to be highly recommended. Over the course of this book we'll look at some important characteristics to take into consideration when designing a governance process, modifying an existing one, or implementing a standard one.

AGILE IS A PROCESS, NOT A PROJECT

If you do currently have a governance process in place it will probably be a form of **project** governance. According to the PMI definition, projects are *"a temporary endeavor undertaken to produce a unique product or service"*. Agile is, on the contrary, a repeatable process, and not a project. Agile has operationalized certain aspects of software development and that affects the ways that project management disciplines can be validly applied to Agile.

A book that gave me much solace when I, as an experienced Project Management Institute certified project manager, was first introduced to Agile was "A Software Project Manager's Bridge to Agility" (Sliger & Broderick, 2008). I've since had the opportunity to hear Michelle Sliger at a Project Management Institute (PMI) seminar, and I think this book does a great service both to project management, and to Agile. It provides context for project managers when they first look at the tools and techniques of Agile. By showing how traditional project management and Agile share fundamental principles, it demonstrates how project manager's skills are transferable to Agile.

However, the idea that you can map various project management activities and processes to Agile, treating Agile as a just another project methodology, is a simplification. As a continuous process, Agile is **not** a project. Treating Agile as if it was a project leads directly to assumptions about how project management tools, techniques, and processes should be actually applied in practice to an established Agile process, Traditional project governance activities are perpetuated that are counter-productive in an Agile environment. I have identified some root cause of these problems that we will explore in the upcoming sections. These are:

1. Defining the solution too early.
2. Making decisions at the wrong time.
3. Still requiring Waterfall artifacts.

Treat Actual Projects as Projects

The exception to the dictum of "Agile is not a project" is when your Agile development process is actually being asked to manage a project! I encountered a situation recently where a large-scale infrastructure project was assigned to our Agile development teams. Large-scale infrastructure projects are not the same as Agile software development! I realized that adjusting the governance accordingly was going to be important for both the sanity of the teams and the success of the infrastructure project. The teams wanted to keep the rhythm of sprints and other cadences going, and to keep project management at a minimum. With the help of the IT Manager we managed the infrastructure project as a distinct project. We instigated a Work Breakdown Schedule and Gantt chart that we used to manage the overall backlog and priorities. We employed traditional rolling-wave planning which provided a semblance of agility, and the teams executed that backlog within their sprints. Although it had some semblance to Agile because the teams themselves were working on stories within sprints, it was still a project, and not an Agile process.

Note: Although Agile is not a project methodology, for want of another word I have used the word "project" to refer to discrete software development initiatives throughout this book. I apologize for the ambiguity, but I felt that departing from using the word 'project' would be ultimately more confusing to you, the reader.

The Problem Of Defining
The Solution Too Early

What happens if the Business forms an idea of what it wants to build early on during market strategy or product roadmap formulation? In other words, what happens if we start by focusing on "requirements" rather than the market problem itself? If we aren't careful these early requirements become more and more entrenched as the project goes through the elaboration and gate process. Then, as the original assumptions become less and less valid, the business justification increasingly becomes a fiction created to defend the original assumption. Instead of actually describing the problem, the market problem statement increasingly becomes just a self-referential re-wording of the originally (assumed) user "requirements".

SYMPTOMS

1. Conflicts and tension are the norm as new information is ignored and changes are vetoed.
2. Many participants become disenfranchised as they begin to realize that the requirements are not correct but are unable to stop the inevitable march to production.

IMPLICATIONS

- The wrong, or at least a sub-optimal, product will be built that will not achieve the hoped for business goals. Agile alone will not solve this problem, and by using Agile as an excuse to accelerate the rush to production, it may even make it worse.

- The symptoms are amplified after the development teams have gone Agile because Agile stresses the importance of the customer and the principle of collaborative problem solving. In the face of this contradiction, talented people in the value stream become demotivated and cease to produce their best work, or leave the organization altogether.

ROOT CAUSES

1. Problems are initially inevitably poorly thought through and defined. It takes substantial effort to dig down to the real problem or root cause, and this shouldn't be done early in the value stream.
2. The change management process is onerous and therefore resistance to change is strongly entrenched in the decision-making process.
3. Accountability and responsibility are not transferred down the value stream. The loudest voice or the highest paid person in the office is allowed to determine a solution that they have become entrenched in defending.

1. Problems are Initially Poorly Specified

Charles Kettering [engineer and inventor 1876-1958] famously said, "a problem well stated is a problem half solved." I would argue that he understated the case because I have frequently found that a problem well stated is a problem that is almost completely solved! This is because in order to state the problem well you first have to have a deep understanding of the possible solutions. The Agile PMO understands this, and is on the lookout for what we call "badly problemed solutions". A badly problemed solution might express itself as something like "The problem is that we don't have email alerts" (see insert "When an Expert Isn't An Expert"). However, if you think about it, this isn't actually a problem, it's a 'solution in disguise'. We know this because it can be rephrased as: **"The solution** (*to some as yet undefined problem*) **is to have email alerts."** Another common example of a poorly defined problem is the 'symptom in disguise'. So something like "The problem is that the wheel squeaks", can be rephrased as **"A** symptom *(of an as yet undefined problem)* **is that the wheel squeaks"**. I will talk about this in more detail in section III, under 'Analyzing Problems'.

When an Expert Isn't an Expert

I recently came across an example of the destructive effects of confusing a solution with a problem. It involved an in-house subject matter expert who was also the project's executive sponsor. Based on his own personal experiences, he had lobbied hard for a feature to send out email alerts. However, when the business analysts researched the problem in depth they realized that the actual issue was that the system did not display changes that had occurred since they last logged in. Generating a log of emails (an inbox) and providing a log of changes is essentially the same thing, but the executive was adamant and so insisted on his original supposition of an email-only solution without displaying a change log at all. By stymying iterative elaboration in this way, the issue degenerated into a power struggle between the executive sponsor, the product manager and the business analysts. It ended up doing untold damage to trust and cooperation throughout the value stream. Everyone ended up miserable - especially the end users who were left with only a partial solution to their actual problem.

---

2. Change Management Process Is Onerous

It is a common characteristic of change management processes that they have an objective to minimize change because change is considered expensive. Lean and Agile techniques are intended to reduce the cost of change by utilizing progressive elaboration and iteration, but if the change management process has not been adjusted to recognize this, then these advantages of Agile are largely wasted.

3. Accountability and Responsibility Are Not Transferred

Highly related to - and often a cause of - defining the problem too early is to not allow accountability of the solution to flow down the value stream. Everyone who touches the market problem and the proposed solution alters them. They are altered by the executives adjusting for corporate, strategic, and tactical constraints; by product managers planning the roadmap into phased milestones; by user researchers taking into consideration the actual workflow; and by developers as they encounter technical limitations. This change is good, and is the natural result of new information being added along the value stream.

Unfortunately, changing the purpose of a feature can be particularly troubling for value stream participants – especially those upstream who might believe that they own, or are ultimately responsible for, the end product and hence believe they have veto power. On the other hand, if we create alignment throughout the value stream, and then trust the professionals that we have hired to do their job, much of these problems can be avoided.

How the Solution is Altered by Value Stream Participants

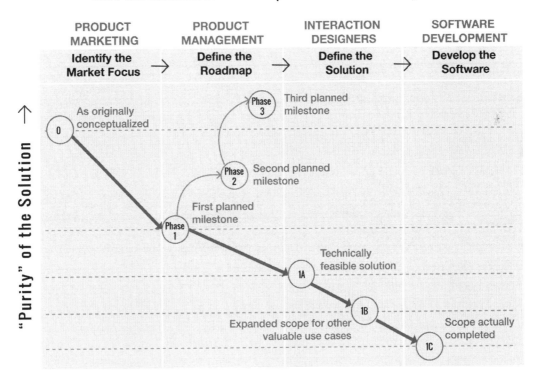

- Compared to the original concept (0), the first planned milestone (Phase 1) appears to product marketers as not enough to make a difference in the market – so they might complain that it is not worth releasing.

- Architects determine the first planned milestone (Phase 1) to be infeasible so an alternative technically feasible solution is designed (1A). Product managers might complain that the solution isn't what they wanted.

- The interaction designers discover additional valuable, use cases that could be solved (1B), or discover that the actual problem isn't as was initially identified. Product marketers and managers might complain that that isn't the problem they wanted addressed.

- Inevitably perhaps, the final, completed solution (1C) doesn't include all the features that were intended because the team ran out of time. The product owner wants the team to 'work harder' to get the full scope into the time-box.

The Problem Of Making Too Many Decisions

What happens when we make too many decisions, too fast? If we change priorities often we do not give time for the Agile teams to be successful. This problem arises when the organization is tactically rather than strategically focused. Sometimes this is because one or more dominant customers are allowed to significantly dictate the development priorities. Sometimes this is because internal departments such as Customer Support are demanding tools and support from the development teams. There may also be sales-related requests for demos or prototypes for the latest industry conference or major prospect. Although the product owner controls the sprint and is able to prevent mid-sprint changes, from sprint to sprint the project priorities are largely out of their control and are subject to change quickly and randomly.

SYMPTOMS

1. There never seems to be enough time to finish a feature properly. The team never actually goes back to iterate on a previously completed feature. There is always another fire to put out, or another urgent request that has priority.
2. Teams are often working on multiple initiatives at once.
3. If business analysts need to work ahead of the team, they often find that they have been working on the 'wrong' thing because while they were researching yesterday's top priority, the priority has changed. This results in large Work-in-Progress queues of stories that are stuck in analysis.

4. Organizational tension is high because there is continuous competition at the management level to get projects to the top of the priority list. Priorities are often determined by the last person to speak, the squeakiest wheel, or the highest paid person in the room at the time.

IMPLICATIONS

- Completion dates are difficult to estimate and often missed because parallel project development and changing priorities lead to unreliable completion dates. The harder the team works, the worse the situation becomes.
- Strategic initiatives never seem to get done because new tactical priorities keep supplanting them.
- There is waste in the form of the effort invested in fleshing out requirements and stories that will never be developed.

ROOT CAUSES

1. Inability to say "No!" to proposed initiatives or feature requests.
2. A belief that Agile implies that priorities change all the time.
3. There is inadequate understanding of the Agile principle of "serial delivery".

1. Inability To Say No

I've been talking so far about the dangers of having "too much" governance. However, I've also found many instances of the opposite case – too little governance. There is a delicate balance in how much oversight the software development process needs. Too much and you stifle the product manager. Too little and the product manager gets buried. The lack of a formal decision-making framework doesn't mean that decisions won't be made; it just increases the probability that the decisions made will be bad ones.

Time and time again we see that the difference between a well-executed strategy and relative chaos is that a good strategy defines what will **not** be worked on, and not just what will. If governance is implemented with a mindset of **exclusion**, then we will be very mindful of when unintended work is being performed and will have the processes in place to 'just say no'.

2. A Belief That Agile Implies That Priorities Change All The Time

As Agile begins to become established within the organization we sometimes find that management begins to emulate the cry from the Technology department for light, flexible planning. However, light flexible planning at the software creation stage should not be an excuse for little or no planning at the management levels. Because hardly any technology project can be completed from inception to deployment in a single sprint, a sprint is **not** the planning cycle time that the rest of the organization should be working to. The lead and cycle times between (1) when decisions are made, (2) when the work is done, and (3) when the final product is deployed, will tell you the frequency of change that your development processes can comfortably support. For optimal productivity the timing of new decisions should match the software delivery cadence. If priorities are changing faster than the delivery cadence then it is inevitable that waste will be generated.

3. Inadequate Understanding Of The Principle Of Serial Delivery

A core principle of Agile 'flow' is that the optimal strategy is to only do one thing at a time so that you deliver value in small batches. This is serial delivery. It is not hard to understand that if we have two projects that will each take one month, that if we work on both of them in parallel we will only be able to deliver them both in two months time. However, if we first complete one project, and then work on the other, we will be able to deliver the first one in only one month's time, while the second project will still be delivered in the same two months as before. This is self-evidently a better outcome because the first project is delivered one month earlier and therefore can start adding value earlier, while the second is not delayed.

In practice, serial delivery can be very hard to achieve. Under weak governance it is often politically more expedient to work on ten 'number one priorities' at once than to actually prioritize the ten projects to work on sequentially. If the organization is in reactive, fire-fighting mode, it is often significantly more palatable to be able to say that you are currently working on everything.

Having said that, the inability for the organization to deliver serially is not always purely a management or governance issue. Technical considerations may also come in to play if Agile teams are specialized resources that cannot focus on a single project, but must be allocated to several projects at once.

The Problem Of Requiring Waterfall Artifacts

What happens if the Business asks for a project plan that is similar in depth, complexity and detail as the Waterfall plans they used to receive before the software development team went Agile? Perhaps before projects can be approved a budget is required - and therefore schedules, scope and detailed resourcing plans are needed. The concern with requiring detailed project plans upfront is that we will need more up-front work to be done than Agile can easily accommodate. If it is taken to extremes, this will cause Agile to fail altogether.

SYMPTOMS

1. Management constantly demands more detail, resulting in a great deal of upfront effort and time spent by the teams on analysis and planning.
2. Project planning generates two plans. One plan is created for management purposes while another, separate, plan is used for Agile development.
3. Agile practices are increasingly compromised in an attempt to serve a rigid, document-centric governance process.
4. Executive management is increasingly viewed by the technologists as being unsupportive of the Agile process and the technologists are increasingly seen as uncooperative and disconnected from the 'real business needs' by executive management.

IMPLICATIONS

- A reversion to Waterfall design patterns is likely because static project plans discourage iterative delivery.
- The benefit of reducing wasted work evaporates as more work is performed upfront to feed the governance planning, most of which will be outdated by the time it is ready to be used.
- In extreme cases, Agile is deemed unsuitable and abandoned altogether.

ROOT CAUSES

1. There is a failure to see the product development value stream as a whole. Executives view Agile as something that the Technology department does that does not affect them.
2. Organizational inertia requires the old governance processes are followed, rather than facilitating necessary changes.

1. Failure To See The Whole Value Stream

When Agile is introduced it is often done so at a grass-roots level or at the best, by the Technology managers. Rarely is it seen as the full-scale, organizational, cross-functional upheaval that it really is. However, Agile, as a Technology-driven initiative, is a *downstream* response to an *upstream* problem that is really the product marketing or product management department's problem. Given that the problem is being generated upstream, it follows that Agile itself can only be as truly successful as Product Management lets it be.

Over time I have come to realize that Agile as a framework is *not* actually about software engineering at all. Agile was not created as a result of any problem with actually coding, testing, or deploying software. Adjuncts like eXtreme Programming (XP), Continuous Delivery, and other engineering disciplines indeed focus exclusively on improving code and test quality. However those things could, and do, stand alone. It is not actually necessary to be doing iterative development, sprints, showcases and all the other paraphernalia in order to get the benefits of XP paired programming or continuous integration. So if the problem is just about code quality, then clearly Agile is overkill.

If Agile is not about software engineering, what is it about? It's about software *delivery*. And what is the real problem that we are trying to solve? The real problem is that "those pesky product managers keep changing their minds!" For a long while the counter-measure for this 'unfortunate habit' was to try to force them to not change their minds, and so traditional project management was brought to bear – project charters, project plans, comprehensive up-front designing, and change management control were all intended to tie the Business and the product manager down to a set of decisions, and hence give the development teams a chance to finish projects successfully. This Waterfall process was until recently the most prevalent form of software development.

The track record of Waterfall over the last 30 years has not been stellar. Instead of executing successful projects, projects were often late, over budget, and when they **were** delivered, they often didn't meet 'fit-for-use' criteria. Despite best efforts, none of the strictures of consecutive, phased project management seemed to fix the fundamental problem of "those pesky product managers who keep changing their minds". We now know that this is because product managers were changing their minds not because they are generally indecisive people, but because they had to. Product managers are not clairvoyant. They changed their minds as a result of two primary influences – uncertainty and flux. *Uncertainty* because no matter how much market research you try to do, and how much business analysis you do, it is just a fact that building useful, valuable software is difficult. At the end of the day, because the market cannot be directly observed, the market is essentially unknowable, and the best we can do is to form hypotheses and then test those hypotheses in the market. *Flux* because it takes time to bring software to market, and during that time there is constant change in the market, in customer behavior, and in technology.

Because change is endemic to software development, it needs to be managed. However, if the governance process does not recognize the need to accommodate the inevitability of change, then the responsibility to manage that change falls solely and entirely on the Agile software development process itself. Unfortunately, Agile is not capable of carrying the whole value stream in this way. The situation is not sustainable and so will ultimately doom any hope of the long lasting success of Agile.

Organizational Inertia

Change is famously difficult. There is an allegory of a troupe of gorillas and a ladder. Thirty gorillas are in a cage, with a ladder. At the top of the ladder is a banana. Whenever one of the gorillas attempts to climb the ladder to reach the banana, the whole troupe is sprayed with water. Soon the gorillas start attacking any who start to climb the ladder. Attempts to climb quickly cease. New gorillas that are introduced to the troupe are quickly attacked if they attempt to climb and so they learn not to do so. The interesting thing is that even if you remove the banana and eventually swap out the entire troupe, the organizational memory will remain and the ladder will not be climbed. Even though the banana and spraying has long been forgotten, gorillas will still attack each other for attempting to climb the ladder. The organizational practice remains long after the reason for it is gone. Our old governance processes might be like that too, with ceremonies still being performed and artifacts still being requested even though the reasons have been forgotten, and were perhaps made redundant long ago.

Having an outdated governance process that no longer serves the needs of the decision-making process is, at the very least, a distraction. Although this distraction can be minimized if governance is just seen as 'something we have to do' (while the real planning is done through less formal, more Agile, means) it still constitutes pure waste. In contrast to common governance practices, an Agile process does not need much more than a cursory project plan. Risk management, the communication plan, the work breakdown schedule (task list or Gantt chart), the resourcing plan (project team roles and responsibilities), and the budget will have all been operationalized within the chosen Agile methodology that you adopt, and as such do not need to be re-iterated within Agile governance artifacts. Indeed, having these sections in your governance templates can be damaging as it sends a signal to your Agile teams that you are looking to add unnecessary overhead – and are trying to solve a problem that has already been solved.

AGILE GOVERNANCE

cadence

★ ensures alignment across value stream

★ supports just-in-time, serial delivery of AGILE process

> **Balance decisions across cadences**
> annual budgets ⚡ sprints ⚡ product goals
> Match the size of the decision w length of the cadence

★ DELAY solutions till last responsible moment

★ Upstream _and_ downstream processes to work
at same time as TAKT time

GIVE TIME FOR DECISIONS TO BE EXECUTED

perpetual planning

→ AGILE is not anti-planning...it's constant planning

→ "Plan the work, work the plan" → `OH BROTHA!`

→ The plan is not to be "WORKED"... it's useful reference

point to reference and measure current assumptions

document _(the verb)_

☆ Write stuff down

☆ Capture **prevailing assumptions** at the time

☆ **Deep think** by writing it down

☆ Create **transparency**

ACCOUNTABILITY

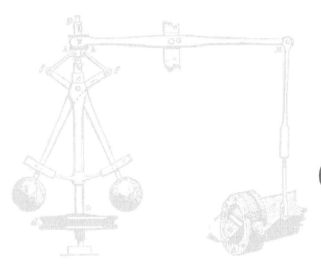

II. Agile Governance

Definition of Agile Governance

Agile is a software development framework within which there are several conformant methodologies, practices, and techniques. Examples of such methodologies include Scrum, Kanban, Scrumban, DSDM and eXtreme Programming. Agile methodologies tend to be elaborative, iterative, time-bound and cadenced. In contrast, the Agile governance that we are talking about here is **not** such a methodology. This book is not about 'governance-that-is-Agile'. 'Governance-that-is-Agile' would be governance performed in an elaborative, iterative way conforming to Agile principles. Although it is perfectly possible to adapt principles from the Agile framework and apply those to the discipline of governance, that is not the primary focus of this book.

Instead, we'll talk about Agile governance as a governance approach that **supports an Agile software development methodology**. I believe this is an important distinction because Agile does not exist in a vacuum. Agile is just one part of a larger value stream. If the rest of the value stream is not supportive in terms of the types of inputs provided, or is not able to consume the outputs produced by Agile, then Agile will fail some or all of its objectives. Therefore Agile governance isn't waste nor unnecessary overhead: it is on the contrary **essential to** the collaborative, iterative Agile process. Management and teams can't change a plan effectively if they don't know what the plan was in the first place, and they can't collaborate and interact over time and distance if they don't document intents, evidence, and decisions.

Agile governance primarily ensures alignment across the value stream. It also helps to appropriately utilize the Agile process. It is a framework for governing the product development value stream in a way that supports the just-in-time, serial delivery needs of an Agile process.

Succeeding With Cadences

Is it possible that because software development takes time, that too much change at the wrong time, can generate as much, if not more, waste than no change at all? Is this "Agile heresy"? One Agile doctrine that I think is often under-emphasized is that the decision points should be as discrete as possible - *make the decision, then give time for the decision to be executed, then evaluate, then make another decision.* This is just a Lean "Plan-Do-Check-Adjust" cycle. On the contrary, if we believe that Agile requires teams to be instantly responsive to change we may conversely think the inability to change quickly (without waste) is indicative of somehow being *un-Agile*. However, maybe we should wonder if Agile itself has limitations to the extent of change it can handle? Indeed, Agile recognizes such limitations, and these limitations are why we have cadences in Agile. A cadence is a regular cycle such as a sprint. We know from Scrum that whereas changes from one sprint to the next are encouraged, during the sprint itself significant changes are strongly discouraged. It is this that we mean when we say that decision points should be discrete.

Agile governance can benefit greatly from leveraging the cadences of sprints and releases, especially where the governance processes touch the software development processes. Release planning is one area in particular where the utilization of cadence can be very important for success.

We would also expect that a well-formed Agile governance process would match the *size* of the decision with the *length* of the cadence. Big decisions that will take time to implement are made infrequently, smaller decisions that take less time can be made more frequently. Let's look at two examples of common cadences, and their decision magnitude – the annual budgeting cycle, and sprints.

- The Annual budgeting cycle is a long cadence that is already institutionalized in many organizations, and is therefore suitable for big decisions like determining what products to work on during the year, and which markets to pursue.
- Sprints are short cadences of one to four weeks. Decisions made during sprint reviews are 'sprint-sized' decisions – for example whether the feature is releasable yet or not, and which stories should be worked on in the next sprint. These decisions will be acted upon within the very next sprint.

If they are already established in the organization, the annual budgeting cycle and sprints are natural decision cadences that should be taken advantage of. However, there is a big time gap between the annual plan and a biweekly or monthly sprint, and it is likely that the Business will need to make decisions in the interim. The more we formalize the timing of those interim decisions, the greater success we set the Agile teams up for.

If the software is being released to market on a regular schedule such as monthly or quarterly, then the release schedule is another natural cadence around which we can create a governance process. If product management needs to have more flexibility we might design a decision making process that was monthly (three decision points per quarter), or every six weeks (two decision points per quarter). Even if we don't have a regular release schedule we can still create an artificial cadence based on monthly management meetings or quarterly steering group meetings.

However it is done, we are trying to meet two objectives:

1. The impact (size) of the decision should match the cadence of the decision. Decisions should not be made for the same team and/or product every month if each decision is going to take three months to execute. If we fail in this, the Agile principle of 'serial delivery' will be broken and the team will find themselves working across parallel initiatives - diffusing their efforts and generally confusing everybody.

2. The timing of the decision should be "at the last responsible moment". Ideally you will have finished, or be finishing, the previous set of work to be able to start this new work almost immediately after the new decision is made.

All this doesn't mean that the decision can't be changed – in fact we expect change – but we try to reduce waste by setting expectations of what changes can be made at what time, and plan the work around that. In Agile, when the decision is changed we should have completed enough of what we ***were*** working on to be able to move on to the new work without waste.

TAKT TIME

A more technical way of expressing concepts of decision cadences is ***the Agile governance process should be leveled to the takt time***. In Lean, "takt" is the frequency at which customer orders arrive. In a well-tuned Lean manufacturing process the factory produces goods at the same average rate as they are ordered (the takt time), and every process within the factory also works at that same rate. If this is the case, then there are no bottlenecks. The equivalent in software development is the frequency at which the Business or product manager asks for new features. Ideally, Agile governance processes operate at the takt time too. If it takes a month to develop a feature, then each of the upstream and downstream design/approval/release processes should also take a month.

In summary, detailed story level changes are made within the iteration, larger story-priority calls are made from iteration to iteration, and feature/market problem changes are made from release to release and from year to year.

Succeeding With Perpetual Planning

A gile is a response to inevitable change, and as we have noted, change is endemic to the software development process. The software development teams in the Technology department need to have the capacity to respond to those changes. However, just because the teams themselves embrace change, doesn't mean that the Business has a license to change its mind arbitrarily, or on a whim. We must still make the best decisions we can, given the information known to us at the time.

Whereas traditional governance serves the need of the Business for stability and predictability, Agile governance serves the need of the value stream to be *elaborative* and *responsive*. In contrast with traditional project management techniques which stress "Plan the work, and work the plan", when General Eisenhower coined the phrase "plans are nothing; planning is everything" he was emphasizing that it is the *process* of planning that is most important for battle: defining objectives, establishing baseline expectations, considering opportunities, evaluating challenges. We recognize, in other words, that "no plan survives first contact with the enemy" (von Moltke the Elder). This is as applicable in software as it is for war.

Although Agile is often seen as being 'anti-planning', in fact Agile software development methodologies encourage constant planning. At the end of every sprint and every release we are re-evaluating and re-planning. The important point is that, like Eisenhower, we are mindful that the plan should only followed as long as it remains relevant and useful, after which point the plan must be abandoned or changed.

FACILITATING PROGRESSIVE ELABORATION

Good Agile governance explicitly encourages (if not actually forces) change through its insistence on progressive elaboration. Done well, progressive elaboration allows us to "fail fast" by being able to identify avenues that are non-productive and to terminate them before spending too much time and effort on them. Done well, progressive elaboration creates a better end product because it allows both micro and macro changes to be made to the plan as new information is presented. As a result, in an Agile governance process we welcome a significant amount of change as the project proceeds down the value stream. Starting with a high level outline, the details are fleshed out through the process of progressive elaboration as we go from initial market problem identification to creating the roadmap, and to eventually designing the solution. Even the high-level strategic plan itself may evolve over time as new information is incorporated as part of the feedback loop from the downstream elaborations.

Following principles of "doing things at the last responsible moment" and iterating, a properly designed Agile governance process will not contain detailed, out of date documents. It will contain living documents that are continuously updated to be always fresh and relevant.

Risk Management and Progressive Elaboration

Risk management is one of the most important aspects of running a successful project. Progressive elaboration is actually a powerful form of risk management and the use of progressive elaboration is what makes Agile such a great dynamic, adaptive risk management system. Most of the more significant risks within software development are handled systemically by the framework itself via iterative, elaborative process: technical risk, scope risk, resource risk and to a certain extent business risk are all managed by the framework in this way.

CAPTURING ASSUMPTIONS ALLOW BASELINING OF PROJECTS

In project management a 'baseline' plan is a plan against which subsequent changes can be measured. The dilemma is how to create a meaningful baseline if the plan is being constantly elaborated and changed? Just as in a traditional governance process, we can baseline whenever the project passes through any sort of gate or review. The difference is that with Agile we are less concerned with the details of the baseline plan than we are with the assumptions behind the plan.

In traditional project management, guesses and assumptions are not central to the plan. On the contrary they are often considered failures of planning that need to be rectified, or are captured just for risk mitigation purposes. In Agile, however, the assumptions constitute the majority of the plan itself. Agile methodologies regularly substitute assumptions for knowledge. This is especially the case early in the process where knowledge is either not immediately obtainable, or would be expensive to gain. By making assumptions, we are avoiding detailed work that will either not be used because the project does not get approved, or will be out of date by the time the project actually begins. The trade-off is that those same assumptions are expected to change - they are not intended to be used as a yardstick for project planning quality and should not be so used. We aren't as interested in knowing how accurate our assumptions were, as we are in knowing what the effect of changing those assumptions has been. In traditional project management where you 'plan the work, and work the plan' the baseline is the original plan to which the project is kept as closely as possible to. Agile does not view the plan as something that should be worked, but rather a useful reference point against which the current set of assumptions and information can be evaluated.

An Upstream Problem – Selling Roadmap 'Futures'

A common situation in software companies with long sales cycles is that the sales teams end up selling features that are on the long-term roadmap instead of the product as it is today. The logic is that by the time the client signs the contract and the product is delivered, those features will actually be in the product.

A few years ago my Product Marketing Vice President came up to me. "I get Agile," he said. "I've worked with Agile teams before, but what I don't get here is why I'm being told by Technology that I can't tell the market what we are delivering in a year. In all the other places that I've worked, the Agile teams have been able to do that." I nod wisely, yes I agreed that other companies say what they intend to work on in the future, and therefore sell stuff that they don't have, and yes, I could see that might be frustrating when trying to sell our product, as yes, we were quite clearly at a (self-imposed) competitive disadvantage, which was detrimental to everyone's - especially the Sales folks' - bonuses (...*sigh!*).

I then went on to point out to this vice president that it wasn't Technology's inability to forecast the future that was at issue. It was his own department that couldn't (and shouldn't) be locking in to a predefined, fully scoped Roadmap. I pointed out to him that every other week he was dealing with unexpected client issues, new priorities that had been established by the latest sales deal, and changing executive priorities. In pushing back on giving set dates and detailed estimates based on 'today's' requirements, Technology was actually doing him a big favor!

It's difficult for people to realize that the enemy is, sometimes, themselves.

Succeeding With Accountability

Having the apparatus to effectively collect, communicate and preserve information is how governance deals with hand-offs between participants that are separated by location, by function, and by time. The goal of Agile governance is to ensure that these hand-offs are highly collaborative and are not 'thrown over the wall'. Traditional governance relies on a static list of artifacts and 'frozen' hand-off documents to gain alignment. Agile governance provides a framework for an ongoing iterative and evolving conversation.

Agile governance artifacts are intended to be interpreted as 'what we knew and thought at the time', and are not definitive statements of fact. Changes to those artifacts are considered a normal part of the process. We do not hold sacred the contents of the artifact or plan, and will abandon it completely if it no longer proves useful.

Rather than moving linearly through the value stream, artifacts will be repeatedly revisited – for example the market strategy may be revised during annual budgeting, and the annual budget might be revised during release planning. Despite this, Agile governance recognizes that the focus and purpose of each stage in the value stream is distinct, and accountability for each stage should be delegated accordingly. Therefore, with hand-offs occurring at the end of each phase, it is more appropriate to think of the value stream as a spiral. In this spiral all stakeholders are represented at all times and the work proceeds collaboratively. In "Principles of Product Management Flow" (Reinertsen, 2009) Reinersten argues that the path though a product management [governance] process should not be linear, but should be thought of as a packet being routed through a telecommunications network. The packet should be routed not according to a predetermined path, but in a way optimized for that packet, visiting nodes as they become free, and as they become relevant.

Agile Governance Is Spiral in Nature

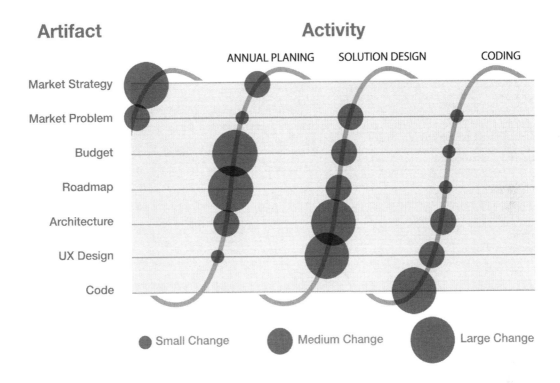

Whether envisaged as a spiral or a network the Agile governance process certainly shouldn't be seen as linear. Each rotation around the spiral, or jump to a node in the network, moves the market problem through the value stream, bringing different artifacts and functional specialties to the fore. Those functional specialties should be made accountable for that stage's respective deliverables.

Indicated below in the sample accountability matrix is how accountability might change throughout the value stream. The specific needs of the organization, the skills and temperaments of the people have in those positions, the size of the group, and many other factors will determine whether you follow this matrix closely or not.

Sample Accountability Matrix

	Executive	Product Marketer	Product Manager	Business Analysts	Agile Team
Identify Market Problems		A	C	C	
Identify Market Segments		A	C		
Develop 3-5 Year Strategy	A	R	C		
Create Annual Roadmap	C	C	A	C	C
Create Solution Design	I	I	C	A	C
Code & Test			I	C	A
Go-to-Market Strategy	C	A	C		
Launch Product		C	A		

A = 'Accountable', R = 'Responsible', C = 'Consult', I = 'Inform'

agile governance
TECHNIQUES

√ Adapt traditional activities to agile ways of thinking

√ Avoid vague comparatives   "about" *over* "more than..."

√ Avoid 'bad goals' ... biz outcomes are beyond your control

watch for **SOLUTIONS** *and* **PROBLEMS** in **DISGUISE**

SPIN

focus on the problem
the solution will appear
Stating the problem well
takes real work

consider **COST of dELAY** to prioritize projects

Jobs delayed most are jobs w lowest cost of delay

IF NOTHING ELSE
APPLY AGILE BEYOND TECH
UNDERSTAND CADENCE
DEMAND MANAGEMENT
to DO LESS and COMPLETE MORE

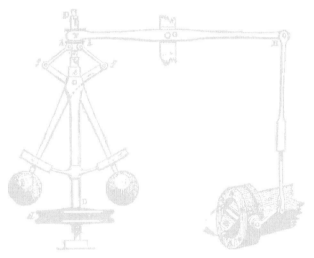

III. Agile Governance Techniques

Resourcing & Scheduling Under Uncertainty

Very often the Agile PMO will have to be creative when reconciling the needs of longer term planning with the need for the teams to remain Agile. It is particularly unlikely that the budgeting process will have much flexibility in it, and both the Technology and Product Management departments will be expected to provide information to allow the organization to meet its fiduciary responsibilities. "We'll only decide that at the last responsible moment" isn't an answer that your Chief Financial Officer wants to hear during the budget cycle.

The Agile governance process will therefore need to be prepared to produce a schedule and resource plan as part of the annual planning process. Despite the fact that executives may be expecting a Gantt chart with resources and dates attached as they were used to under a Waterfall process, it might be unwise to ask your Agile teams to produce this. I have seen teams struggling to define the scope to a detailed, estimatable story level in order to provide the level of 'committable' detail that was seemingly being demanded by the Business. This is ultimately a futile exercise and causes much frustration with Agile teams. Happily, there are better ways. With some imagination it is possible to adapt traditional project management activities to the new Agile way of thinking.

A top-down approach to long-range estimation (for annual planning purposes) that I've seen work is to use T-Shirt sizes of Small, Medium, Large, Extra-Large and so on, to initially estimate the project list. This can be done extremely quickly just with the product manager and a few Technology managers or architects. By reviewing the entire project list, we then convert the T-Shirt sizes to sprints by making an informed guess as to how many sprints the T-Shirt sizes translate to, based on historical velocity. This is a type of estimation similar to what the Scaled Agile Framework (Leffingwell, 2011) refers to as 'Normalized' velocity.

For example, 'Small' might be one sprint, 'Medium' 4 sprints, and 'Large' 8 sprints. You can use doubling like this, or you can follow a Fibonacci pattern where each size is about 1.5 times larger than the previous one. That decision will depend on the nature of your projects, and how similar or dissimilar they are. The goal at this stage is only to get order-of-magnitude accuracy. At the end of this exercise you should have a list of projects with an estimate of effort expressed as the number of sprints next to each one. This is a simple, raw estimate that necessarily will be extremely uncertain. We take this estimate as our 'low' estimate because developers and product managers are notoriously optimistic.

To accommodate uncertainty we now add an upper limit to the estimates. There are two sources of uncertainty that may derail the plan and that we can explicitly model. The first source of uncertainty is scope. How vague, open, or ambiguous is the scope? How likely is it that the work is broader than it appears now? Experience in similar projects and in the group's intuition of the project will give you a margin of error of the 'maximum' scope as some multiple of the low estimate. The second source of variability is the technical risk. Technical risk reflects the uncertainty of the amount of actual effort that may be required to achieve the scope. The original T-Shirt estimates assumed a certain level of effort based on an expected level of technical complexity. Now we should think about a reasonable 'worst case' scenario. How much more effort might possibly be required for the same basic scope? Twenty percent? Fifty percent? One hundred percent? Make an assumption for each one of the projects.

Multiplying *scope* uncertainty and ***technical risk*** uncertainty together will give the ***overall worst case*** buffer, which is the buffer for when the project proves to be both technically more difficult and broader in scope than originally conceived. For example, if the scope might be 20% broader, and the technical risk is such that 50% more effort might be required, then the total buffer is 80% ($1.20 \times 1.50 = 1.80$). So it follows that if the original estimate was 5 sprints, then the upper limit is 9 sprints (5×1.80). This calculation can be made for all the projects in the portfolio.

How do we combine all our projects into a single, annual plan? If we just sum the low estimates, then our total estimate for the whole portfolio would be too low, as we would have not taken risk into account. On the other hand if we summed the worst-case estimates our total estimate would be much too high because not all projects will be that complicated or run that late. To solve this, we calculate the 'expected time to completion' as being the low estimate for each project plus some adjustment. The 'expected time to completion' (ETC) is the time that the project will finish on or before with a 50% probability. The worst-case scenario we somewhat arbitrarily but conveniently define as having a probability of 10% of occurring (i.e. it is the 90th percentile). On a Weibull (1.7) distribution the 90th percentile occurs two standard deviations above the low estimate.

The Weibull Distribution

A Weibull probability distribution function has been found to be a more realistic model for project completion dates than a Normal distribution. Weibull distributions are used to predict the failure rate of mechanical components over time, among many other applications. The Weibull distribution is bounded by zero, and can be highly skewed.

Weibull distributions are defined by two parameters. The alpha parameter defines the shape of the distribution, and the beta parameter defines the scale. The beta parameter is uninteresting because it just describes absolute magnitude, but the alpha parameter is very interesting because it changes the shape of the curve. When the alpha parameter is set to about 1.7 the distribution has an interesting property: the distance from the most likely observation (the high point of the probability function) to the 90th percentile is about two standard deviations, and the expected observation (50th percentile) is one half a standard deviation from the most likely.

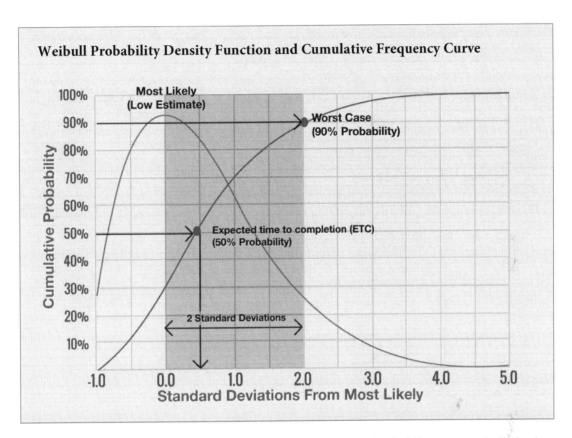

Weibull Probability Density Function and Cumulative Frequency Curve

Therefore, assuming that the project estimate does indeed follow a Weibull (1.7) distribution (see insert), the adjustment we need to make to calculate the ETC is to add half a standard deviation to the low estimate. This is easily calculated as being quarter of the difference between the low and the high estimate.

Creating estimation ranges like this at the individual project level can be used to deprioritize a highly risky/unknown project in favor of a safer project or to create a research task to gather more information to reduce the level of uncertainty. It can also be used to sum projects to create a responsible annual plan. However, if I am using project buffers individually like this, I often will find it more prudent to use a *full* standard deviation as the adjustment instead of just *half* a standard deviation. By doing this, I raise the probability that the individual project will be completed on time from 50% to 70%.

This is even easier to calculate than the ETC because it is simply the mid-point between the high and low estimates, instead of just a quarter of the way between!

Alternatively, instead of padding each individual project a slightly more robust scheduling technique for the projects taken all together is to calculate a separate portfolio schedule buffer. A schedule buffer for 90% confidence is derived by combining the individual project standard deviations. Given the assumptions above, and because project completion times are independent of each other, the portfolio standard deviation is calculated by halving the difference between the ETC and worst case estimate for each project, squaring the result, summing across all projects, and taking the square root. Doubling the result will give the 90% confidence limit that we can use as the schedule buffer (Cohn, 2006). The annual plan is based on the aggregate low estimates, plus the portfolio schedule buffer.

Mike Cohn and others assume the original estimate is the ETC estimate, rather than the low estimate, otherwise my treatment is the same as other writers on the subject. It should matter little in practice, but you might like to demonstrate that to yourself.

PROJECT BUDGETING

In my experience there is a wrong way and a right way to do project budgeting in an Agile organization. The first way is a bottom-up approach where we take the projects that we want to execute during the year, we estimate them, rank them by attractiveness using an financial or multivariate scoring system, and then approve the projects that above a particular threshold.

The second way is a top-down approach, in which we examine the strategic goals, decide which projects will have the biggest impact on achieving those goals, and then decide how much you are willing to spend on each based on a rough T-shirting of effort.

The second, top-down, method is vastly superior to the first from an Agile perspective. For one thing, it is very cheap to get an 'order of magnitude' for each of your projects, because it takes very little scoping and estimating. Secondly, because you are only focusing on projects that are strategic or clearly beneficial in nature, you can save time and emotional energy by never considering all the other projects that don't fall into this category. Because many annual plans continue to be made in the traditional, bottom up way, teams waste lots of up-front effort in doing detailed analysis and estimation, while still often failing to meet the goals of delivering on time and on budget.

Even highly competent leadership teams can be misled by their experiences with Gantt charts and traditional (waterfall) project management to ask the wrong questions – and worse, to misunderstand the answers. The classic book "Waltzing With Bears" (DeMarco & Lister, 2003) discusses the particular myopia of over-emphasizing costs, and under-emphasizing benefits when doing project planning.

Evaluating Projects
By Cost of Delay

All governance processes require some way to evaluate and rank projects. Let's examine three such ways. First we'll recap the traditional capital allocation metrics based on discounted cash flows, then we'll look at multivariate ranking models, and finally we'll take a look at the "cost of delay" which is, by way of contrast, an opportunity cost framework.

DISCOUNTED CASH FLOW

We know that there are lots of issues with using traditional discount cash flow metrics for capital allocation because they just weren't designed to deal with software projects. Return on Investment (ROI), Net Present Value (NPV), and Internal Rate of Return (IRR) are all discounted cash flow methods that measure slightly different aspects of the value of a series of cash flows. They are calculated by estimating inflows and outflows of cash that your project is anticipated to consume or generate, and then applying a discount rate to take into consideration future flows that are less valuable due to inflation and interest costs, or because they are riskier (more uncertain). The result of such calculations can be meaningfully compared with other alternatives such as the return on bonds of a similar duration, and they can be used to compare and rank projects by attractiveness. Many people find these calculations particularly attractive because they appear to be objective measures of value.

I believe that it is not appropriate to use capital allocation metrics for the evaluation of Agile software development projects because software project decisions are not like deciding whether to rent or buy a house, or to build a manufacturing plant in Indonesia or China. Consider these several differences:

- **Interdependence**. Agile software development projects are very often interdependent. Any one market release, any one feature, cannot be distinguished from all of the other components that make up the product, and so whereas the cost might be able to be calculated precisely, the resultant positive cash flows are little more than a guess. We can't really separate a project to create a premium feature, from one to enhance the supportability of the feature in the market. The former might have measurable sales, but the latter might enable scaling to support all those new customers or might prevent a cataclysmic event that could shut down your entire business.

- **Irrelevant Costs.** For software projects the developments costs are not particularly significant. If the project is successful there is often an order of magnitude difference between the costs and the benefits. It matters little at the end of the day if a project costs $100,000 or $500,000 if it nets the company $5,000,000.

- **Meaningless Rates of Return**. A successful product will likewise exhibit several orders of magnitude difference between the costs of capital and the risk-free rate, leading to ridiculous IRR results. How do you compare a project that is returning 400% with a risk-free USD Treasury rate of 0.12% at the time of writing (January 2014)?

- **Highly Uncertain Cash Flows.** The uncertainty of both the magnitude and the size of incoming cash flows mean that any calculation quickly becomes a meaningless reiteration of the wild guesses that went into the forecasts. We are notoriously bad at forecasting. It is not uncommon for estimates of project value to differ by a factor of 50 between individuals asked to evaluate them.

- **Uncertain Terminal Values.** Software has an indeterminate life span. The terminal value (the value after you give up forecasting cash flows at the end of three or five years) can be a considerable part of the overall calculation, but ends up being just another wild guess on top of a guess owing to the uncertainties of both the residual value and of the actual longevity of the software.

MULTIVARIATE RANKING

Because of the weaknesses of financial metrics, multivariate ranking is another technique that has wide support. It is very simple to explain, and simple to perform. Each project is scored across multiple desirable attributes. The scores are then summed across all the attributes to provide a total for each project, which can then be used as a ranking.

Because the attributes that are being considered can be qualitative as well as quantitative, subjective as well as objective, using this type of ranking system is extremely robust. Continuous metrics (such as financial ones) can be converted into ranks or normalized scores. Scoring systems such as 1 to 10, or even simple 'high, medium, low' scoring systems can be also used. If only two attributes are being considered it can be presented as a scatter-chart or grid (the simplest form being the two-by-two grid). Most two-by-two grids in common usage have some sort of reward as one dimension, and a risk measure as the other. Other dimensions can also be incorporated on the chart by changing the size, color or shape of marker, creating bubble-charts.

The robustness of multivariate ranking makes it suitable for use in variety of situations throughout the value stream. Here are just few examples of usage, with examples of typically used multivariate dimensions:

- **Competitive Assessment**. *Dimensions*: investment, impact to customer.
- **Opportunity Scoring**. *Dimensions*: strategic alignment, competitive landscape, investment, impact to customer.
- **Project Evaluation**. *Dimensions*: strategic alignment, financial impact **OR** strategic alignment, product advantage, market attractiveness, ability to leverage core competencies, technical feasibility, reward vs. risk.

THE COST OF DELAY

I was first formally introduced to the concept of cost of delay in "The Principles of Product Development Flow" (Reinertsen, 2009). The cost of delay is a financial calculation that, unlike others such capital allocation metrics such as return on investment (ROI), net present value (NPV), payback period, and internal rate of return (IRR), attempts to measure the opportunity cost of time-to-market. The cost of delay is the opportunity cost of **not doing** the project. It is measured in cost per cycle time. A sprint makes a good enough common cycle time, so we can think of the cost of delay in terms of "dollars per sprint". Agile governance can use the cost of delay to optimally prioritize and schedule projects in the roadmap backlog by using the 'weighted-shortest-job-first' (WSJF) principle.

To maximize the economic benefit of a portfolio of projects the sequencing of projects should consider both the cost of delay of each project and the amount of time that the project takes to develop. The sequence of projects that will produce the best total return will prioritize projects with the highest cost of delay per sprint.

To take an example: if a support and maintenance project will save your support team $250 per week after it is implemented, then for every two week sprint this project is delayed, the overall value of the project will be reduced by $500. The cost of delay is therefore $500 per sprint. That money can never be recovered. Compare this with a project for a new feature for which there is a stable market demand. Assume that over the life of that feature $100,000 in sales is expected. If the total value of $100,000 will be reaped regardless of the feature being released in a month or it being released in a year, the cost of delay for that feature is zero. You should do the support project first, because its cost of delay at $500 per sprint is greater than zero.

More often, however, revenue opportunities are extremely sensitive to time. In "Innovation and Entrepreneurship" (Drucker, 1986) he observes that the cost of delay for technology-based innovation can be extremely high. How much revenue will you lose if a competitor beats you to market? How many customers will you have lost forever, and how much will you need to lower your price, in order to compete against an incumbent first mover?

Let's re-examine the project for the new feature. Let's assume that if we release it in a year we will only be able to capture half of the total amount that was previously estimated because we will have to discount the price and some customers will be lost forever to competitors. In this case, we've reduced the value of the feature by $50,000 ($100,000/2) over a period of about 50 weeks. The cost of delay is therefore $1,000 per week, or $2,000 per two-week sprint. Remember that the support project had a cost of delay of only $500 per sprint. Which one should we choose now? The support project will take the development team (the team are the constrained resource) two sprints. The feature project will take the team four sprints. The WSJF for the support project is therefore $500 per sprint divided by two sprints of effort = 250, but for the feature project the same calculation is 500 (2,000/4). You should first do the feature project with a WSJF of 500, and second do the support project with a WSJF of 250.

Consider for comparison that if instead of four sprints, it takes eight for the feature project. Delaying the support project at $250 per week for sixteen weeks would cost $4,000, which is the same as delaying the feature project for four weeks at $1,000 per week. Both projects now have the same WSJF of 250. We would be indifferent between the two projects. In practice, because the savings from the support project are likely to be more certain, and the risk lower, we should probably choose to do the support project first.

The significance of this for Agile governance is that we now have a framework to incorporate *time* into the prioritization decision. For example we can now take into account the opportunity cost of delaying a product to market when deciding to add one more feature to the release. Another welcome attribute of WSJF is that the weighted calculation of WSJF works just as well with comparative story point estimates as it does with actual time estimates. Something that your Agile teams will thank you for!

Using Metrics To Measure Success

It is a management truism that you get what you measure. It is important to know the difference between the various types of metrics, and when to use each one. The four primary types that I like to think metrics fall into, are:

1. **Activity Metrics**. "Is the plan being executed?" *For example:* on time or on budget? (***Project Managers care***)

2. **Direct Results**. "Was the plan successful?" *For example:* solved customers' problem or decreased turnaround times? (***Middle Managers care***)

3. **Business Drivers**. "Did the results of the project have their intended effect on the business drivers?" *For example:* increased market awareness or increased quality perception? (***Executives care***)

4. **Strategic Outcomes**. "Did the drivers lead to the desired outcome?" *For example:* higher profitability or greater market share? (***Shareholders care***)

We'll illustrate these four types using the example of an organization that wishes to reduce the number of clients who are canceling their subscription. They have determined that one of the root causes is that users don't know how to fully utilize the software. The decided strategy is to perform user certification training, with the anticipation that usage rates will increase, and thus leading to a greater ratio of clients renewing.

ACTIVITY METRICS

"Activity metrics" quantify things that are directly under the control of, or directly affected by, the project team members. They measure progress and/or activity. Goals and targets can be easily set for teams or individuals for this type of metric. How many bricks have been laid, pages written, blogs posted? How many calls are being made per day? How many clients contacted? How many training courses are being run? Are we on budget? Are we on schedule? Project Managers measure these to ensure projects are being well executed. For our certification training example, we might track how many users are contacted, how many sign up for training, or how many training sessions are performed. Activity metrics can be used as completion criteria such as "once 500 users have been trained, we can stop the project", or success criteria such as "if we get 250 people trained the project would have paid for itself, and can be considered a success", or both.

DIRECT RESULTS

The direct result of the project or initiative is something that is directly impacted by the project once the project has been completed. It can be appropriate to set goals or targets for the project as a whole using a metric of this type. Governance can use direct results to know if a project has been successful in achieving its purpose. In our example the result we are anticipating is an increase in usage rates following the training, because we intend to train users on features that they might not know existed, and to show them different ways to apply already familiar features.

BUSINESS DRIVERS

Business drivers are statistics that we are attempting to influence with our project or initiative. They are measurable and are directly or indirectly attributable to the direct results of the project. A suitable metric is one that you can measure reasonably accurately and in a timely manner. Senior managers and executives use them to ensure that the business strategy is being executed. They are used to test that projects are having the desired effect. The strategic execution framework of the Balanced Scorecard™ proposes that business drivers relate to customer perceptions of brand, quality, relationships, price, functionality, timeliness and the internal process ones of cost efficiency and asset utilization. In our training example the lever is the 'functionality' lever. We are specifically targeting the perception that the application is not very feature-rich. The training is likely to affect other levers though. It might strengthen the relationship that the customer feels they have with the company, or even their perception of quality. Surveys such as Win/Loss or Net Promoter Scores and other marketing techniques are often employed to gauge the business drivers.

STRATEGIC OUTCOMES

Strategic outcomes capture what the Business is trying to achieve with this strategy. Is the purpose market growth? Increased market share? Increased revenue? Decreased costs? Increased sales? Higher renewal rates? All of these have several things in common:

1. They are not under the control of anyone in the organization.
2. They are lagging indicators.
3. They are influenced by a great many things, the current project being only one.
4. They won't be known until much later, long after the project has finished.

For these reasons, we need to use metrics of this type with great caution. Executives, Board members, and Shareholders use these to ensure that the business strategy is successful ("our training program increased renewals by 3%). Unfortunately for them -

and the project - nobody will know this for at least a year after the project has finished, when retention ratios and revenue from renewals can be calculated. Additionally, because the effect might persist over time or be extremely delayed, so care should be taken when interpreting outcomes for any one project or initiative.

Is The Number Good or Bad?

I was reminded the other day that people unconsciously and automatically interpret and judge any statistic. Is a high capacity utilization desirable or not, what is the correct number? Is a highly variable velocity good, or bad? Are a lot of releases, hot patches and updates good or bad? As Agilists we need measurements in order to control and improve all our processes - but what should be measured, and what do the measurements really mean?

Sometimes you just don't know. Sometimes you have to measure things and see if the statistics tell you a story - and sometimes this can take a while. A team I was coaching decided to track its capacity utilization. The first iteration this was calculated at 73%, and the team was worried that was low. After 6 iterations they identified that utilization was highly variable and random - other statistics were probably more important

This goes against the Agile grain in two ways - in Agile we don't like waste, and measuring for measurements sake appears wasteful ... and also as humans we need to interpret everything ... is that good, or bad ... what does it MEAN?

Sometimes, though, you have to be patient and let the data speak for itself.

Techniques for
Making Decisions

Stage-Gate Framework®, Pragmatic Marketing®, the Balanced Scorecard®, Agile Project Management/DSDM Atern®, and the Scaled Agile Framework® are all established 'new product development' frameworks that have decision-making and project approval components to them. While creating our own Agile governance framework it might therefore be advantageous to examine these decision-making and project approval processes carefully. According to Stage-Gate®, there are two basic different approaches to project approval (1) a bottom-up, project-based approach, and (2) a top-down, portfolio approach. The difference between the two approaches hinges on the relative dominance given between *project gates*, and *portfolio review*s (Cooper, Edgett, & Kleinschmidt, 2002).

Project gates and portfolio reviews remain an important, even vital, part of Agile governance. They are part of the cadence, part of the feedback cycle, and part of the transparency of Agile. Both project gate and portfolio review meetings are discrete moments in time when a decision can be made, and assumptions can be baselined. As checkpoints, they extend and enhance the benefits of documentation. Even if your upstream processes are so highly effective and collaborative that gates and reviews become formal rubber stamps, they are still useful to have as records of fact that will persist into the future. They enable you to gain organizational buy-in, obtain approval to move forward, create an auditable trial, and, unfortunate though it is to mention, occasionally are useful in various "personal risk mitigation" strategies, where a paper trail becomes necessary! So as we can see, Agile governance welcomes both project gates and portfolio reviews!

Unfortunately, as far as Agile decision-making methods go, neither the project gate dominant nor the portfolio review dominant approaches look particularly attractive. It turns out that they both encourage long queues and wasted work. To understand why we need examine them both more closely.

THE PROJECT-GATE APPROACH

In the Project-Gate approach, resourcing and Go/Kill decisions are made predominantly at *project gate*s. During project gate meetings, intensive reviews of a few individual projects are conducted. Decisions concerning those projects are made in the meeting itself. Go/Kill decisions are therefore made in relative isolation, and are based mainly on the singular merits of the individual project under consideration. In this approach the *portfolio review* meetings still happen, but are mostly status report meetings for ongoing projects that have already passed their respective gates.

Characteristics of Project-Gate

- **Poor Resource Allocation.** If there are no free resources at the time of the gate review, then a good project may be approved but not resourced, put on hold, or even canceled. In the first case, having approved projects that are essentially 'unfunded mandates' generates waste and frustration within the whole value stream, and holding up or even canceling a good project with a high cost of delay just because of no resource availability is sub-optimal and even more frustrating.

- **Wasted Work**. Projects are rarely actually 'killed' – decisions are often simply put 'on hold pending further investigation' (come back next month with more detail), or approved 'pending resources being available' (which they often never are). Often the product manager is encouraged to keep moving the project slowly forward, with the consequences of large queues, long cycle times, long lead times, and lots of wasted work when the project is eventually canceled. This becomes increasingly expensive the longer the project is stuck at the gate.

- **Poor Strategic Alignment.** Because projects are being approved one by one it is difficult to keep the overall portfolio aligned with the strategic vision, or to maintain a balance of projects, because a larger view is rarely taken at the portfolio level, given that portfolio reviews are mostly status reports.

THE PORTFOLIO-REVIEW APPROACH.

By way of contrast, with the Portfolio-Review approach, resourcing and Go/Kill decisions are made predominantly during *portfolio review* meetings. During portfolio review meetings all projects are evaluated together, usually by ranking projects using multivariate rankings or financial criteria. Spreadsheets, two-by-two grids and bubble charts are all suitable for this purpose. During the review process, all projects compete against each other for resources. In theory at least, any project, regardless of sunk costs, may be reevaluated and canceled or put on hold at any time. In this approach, project gate meetings still occur for each project, but instead of being venues for Go/Kill decisions as they are in the Project-Gate approach, they are merely status updates for the project. Project status is reviewed to see whether it is proceeding as expected, that there are no significant risks materializing, and that the business justification is still valid for that project. Under this approach, major decisions are not normally made at the project gate unless the project is in real trouble.

Characteristics of Portfolio-Review

- **Good Resource Allocation.** Resource planning is an intrinsic part of the prioritization and approval process, meaning that if a project is approved, resources are assigned to it at the same time. Consequently, "unfunded mandates" are avoided.
- **Good Strategic Alignment.** By reviewing the whole portfolio together the portfolio can be efficiently balanced to align with strategic changes. Portfolio balancing ensures that there is an appropriate blend of projects in the project pipeline. In addition to strategic alignment, projects are typically balanced across several other attributes, including early stage vs. late stage projects, new

development vs. maintenance projects, and high risk/return projects vs. steady growth projects.

- **Wasted Work.** Lots of work across many projects is required in preparation for each portfolio review. Because it is a "survival of the fittest" approach it is not designed to be resource-efficient. On the contrary, resources are expected to be spent on demonstrating that the project is 'the fittest'. Of course, work performed on projects that do not pass the review is wasted work. Even projects that do pass are likely to have had too much work performed on them too early in their life cycle. This work is waste because it will be out of date and will have to be redone when the project actually is ready to be developed.

- **Organizational Friction.** The highly competitive nature of project selection leads to executives and senior managers spending inordinate time lobbying and positioning for their own projects, which often leads to intense organizational discord. There is little or no incentive for senior managers to co-operate, because project selection is a zero-sum game. Additionally, the project teams are not normally invited to the portfolio reviews, the team is not there to defend the project and this can lead to poor decisions, and frustration by the team.

A HYBRID AGILE GOVERNANCE APPROACH

Project gates and portfolio reviews are necessary and useful, but they lead to wasted work and long queues. So how can we design a decision-making approval process that manages queues better? Queues are themselves expensive because each queue consumes management and executive time in discussing, reviewing, and prioritizing it. Additionally, the further the project moves downstream, the more work is invested in it, so the more expensive it becomes to cancel it. We should prevent long downstream queues from forming. Let's see how these two different approaches manage queues.

Queue-Handling of Project-Gate and Portfolio-Review Approaches:

- **Project-Gate** is a *single-unit push* process. It pushes projects one by one into downstream queues. Push-processes cannot manage the queues that they are pushing to downstream of them. They are, however, very suited for controlling work-in-progress. For example, with Project-Gate it is easy to limit the number of projects being worked on within each gate. When a project passes through a business proposal gate, the team that was working on that project can now start the analysis on the next project in their queue (by pulling it).

- **Portfolio-Review** is a *batched queue management* process. A batch of projects is pruned during the portfolio review process. We would expect overall shorter downstream queues compared to Project-Gate, but we have much less control over work-in-progress. In fact, because it is a batch system, Portfolio-Review *encourages* lots of work-in-progress, especially immediately upstream from the review. Incidentally, because it is a batch process, it also encourages the *parallel* development of projects, over the preferred Agile principle of *serial* delivery.

Demand Management and Agile Governance

The purpose of the annual plan is to manage demand for software development for the upcoming year, which it does by managing the annual backlog. As I've described it earlier, the annual planning process is clearly *Portfolio-Review*. Utilizing an annual cadence to manage the large, portfolio-level decisions enables top-down resource assignment to be conducted, and as we now know, Agile governance is much easier when resources are assigned top-down. Among other benefits, top-down resource allocation negates the need for detailed estimation during the planning phases.

Now if the annual plan is a Portfolio-Review approach, then first gate for the Delivery Plan must be a *Project-Gate* Go/Kill decision otherwise we have sacrificed Agility and locked ourselves into the annual plan. Work on the project during the year should be minimized until immediately before that first gate. Once that gate is passed, however, the project is 'full-on', with the objective of completing it as soon as possible. (Milestone gates are covered in the next section on the Delivery Plan template). In this way, by combining a Portfolio-Review approach to manage the annual queue, with a Project-Gate approach to manage the execution of the queue during the year, we are able to achieve serial delivery of the annual plan with low queue-lengths and minimal waste.

However, demand management cannot begin just at the annual planning stage. Because it is Portfolio-Review, the annual plan is itself being fed by an **unmanaged** queue. The cost of this upstream queue can be slightly reduced by focusing only on the market problems and not solution design, and the cost can be further reduced if we convert this queue from an unmanaged to a **managed** queue. The Scaled Agile Framework (Leffingwell, 2011) suggests doing this by placing limits on the number of projects that product marketers/ managers can work on (kanban limits), and on upstream queue sizes. Most of the major product management frameworks such as Pragmatic® and Stage-Gate® use screening and filtering to manage upstream queues, which they do through a series of gate and review processes.

Summary of the Hybrid Agile Decision-Making Approach

Decision-Making Approaches Compared

	Project-Gate	Portfolio Review	Hybrid Agile
Queue Lengths	High	Medium	Low
Lead Times	High	Medium	Medium
Delivery Mode	Serial	Batch	Serial
Wasted Work	Medium	High	Low
Organizational Friction	Medium	High	Low
Strategic Alignment	Low	High	High

A 'hybrid' Agile governance approach for decision-making will rigorously manage upstream queues by (1) extensively utilizing strategically-driven portfolio reviews up to, and including, the annual plan, and (2) applying WIP constraints on product managers and marketers. A Project-Gate approach is taken for the execution of the milestones in order to ensure that we re-evaluate the plan at the last responsible moment, retaining Agility where it is needed most, which is immediately prior to the development phase.

Techniques for Analyzing Problems

Problem-solving is an important skill and major component of product marketing. The Agile PMO, in their role of *process quality assurance*, should be familiar with how problems can be effectively analyzed and communicated. Marketers and product managers should be the ones who are actually performing this work, of course - defining market problems is not one of the PMO's many responsibilities! In order to become familiar with this area we will look at some traps to be aware of when analyzing problems. We will look at two types of poorly defined problems that may get us embroiled into solution design before it is appropriate. This is important because solution design introduces a variety of costs that we would like to delay until "the last responsible moment". We will also look at a documentation technique called SPIN that your product marketers and managers may find helpful to communicate with the development teams.

POORLY DEFINED PROBLEM STATEMENTS

Beware of "symptoms in disguise" and "solutions in disguise" – two types of poorly defined problem statements. As human beings it is all too natural for us to settle on the first, most obvious thing, but often the real root cause or underlying problem is much harder to determine. The Toyota Production System (TPS) - the ancestor of Lean, Agile and all things good - recognizes this and puts a great emphasis on problem identification. Techniques such as "the five why's", A3 Problem solving, and fishbone analysis are all part of the TPS Lean culture aimed at teasing out root causes.

So what are "symptoms in disguise" and "solutions in disguise"? While teaching a group of cross-functional managers about problem solving I realized that there are two types of statements that appear, at first glance, to be perfectly well expressed problems, but on closer inspection are nothing of the sort.

These are:

1. **Symptoms in Disguise.** "Symptoms in disguise" occur when a *symptom* of the problem is mistaken as being the problem itself. If we have flu, then a decongestant medicine will treat a symptom, but it won't cure the flu itself. Doctors are trained to distinguish between symptoms and diseases. In everyday life and in business, we are often not so discerning. As an example, we might decide that "it is a problem that our sales are lower than expected" and therefore we might think the solution is to increase our sales team's efforts. But perhaps our poor sales numbers are a symptom of low quality in our product, or are because a competitor has leap-frogged us. In which case we would merely be treating the symptom of low sales by making our sales teams work harder, rather than the actual root causes of low quality or loss of feature competitiveness.

2. **Solutions in Disguise.** "Solutions in disguise" occur when we express the *solution* to a problem as being the problem itself. In business we see this often: when we complain that "we don't have enough staff" (*implied solution: "hire more people"*) or when we argue that "we lack training" (*implied solution: "pay for more training"*). From these examples, we can see that a "solution in disguise" might in fact be an appropriate solution to the problem - maybe we really do need more staff or more training … but how are we to know that? By framing the problem as a predetermined solution, we have precluded consideration of any other options, and rendered any rational analysis of the underlying root cause of the problem moot.

The Full Refrigerator

To get a better understanding of how tricky problems are to define I often use a simple example – that of a break-room refrigerator. I'm sure you'll agree it is a universal problem with break-room refrigerators that they always seem full!

But wait! Is "the refrigerator is too full" really the problem? On closer inspection, it is at best a *symptom in disguise*. Framed this way, increasing capacity by buying a second fridge, or buying a larger fridge are the implied solutions. Alternatively "the refrigerator is too full" may in fact be a *solution in disguise* (solution: "empty the refrigerator"). We might think to impose limits on the amount each person can keep in the refrigerator, or to clear out the contents daily or weekly.

More considered thought and analysis in our fictitious example reveals actually 60% of the fridge space is being taken up by only four people. We might also discover that these people are vegetarians. The in-house cafeteria only serves meat dishes, and so the four vegetarians have to bring in supplies to make their lunch. In this case, the full refrigerator is a symptom of a sub-optimal cafeteria menu. The solution? Expand the cafeteria menu to include a vegetarian option.

LEVERAGING SPIN TO WRITE PROBLEM STATEMENTS

The upstream processes performed by product marketing and product management are in the 'problem-space' of product development - the space where the problem is defined. The 'solution-space' - where the solution is defined and executed - belongs downstream with the Agile teams. However, even while still in the problem-space it is human nature to leap to solutions before fully understanding the problem. It is all too easy to accidently fail to understand the real problem when we settle for "solutions in disguise" and "symptoms in disguise". We should be mindful that it is never 'obvious' what the problem is. "Stating the problem well" takes real work, which is the type of hard work that we don't want to be doing until we are at the appropriate point in the value stream. This is the point when the possibility that the effort will be wasted is outweighed by the value of knowing the answer. In fact, the Agile governance process recognizes that properly defining the problem and defining the solution will often happen contiguously with each other – the one feeding the other.

A structure that I have found helpful for documenting market needs and high level requirements without stepping too far into the solution-space is the well-established sales model of SPIN: Situation, Problem, Implication, Need-payoff (Rackham, 1988). This sales model takes potential buyers through a clear progression from implied wants to explicit needs, and it is this progression that makes the model so suitable for upstream documentation of a needs-generating process. The purpose of using SPIN within Agile governance is to maintain the isolation between the desired customer benefits, and the technology solution. A trap to avoid when writing a SPIN is making the solution self-referential. It is surprisingly all too easy to write something that can be boiled down to:

- **Situation**: feature 'A' is missing.
- **Problem**: feature 'A' is needed.
- **Implication**: feature 'A' can't be used.
- **Need**: feature 'A'.

In order to avoid mistakes like this, let's take a look at each of the four parts of SPIN – the Situation, Problem, Implication, and Need in more detail.

Situation

The Situation describes the current market and regulatory environment. As a rule Situations shouldn't reference the product or system unless this is some kind of defect fix to an existing function, in which case mentioning the product is of course essential to the Situation. Depending on circumstances, the Situation may take many forms: workflow orientated use cases, historical narrations, industry trend analysis or any other suitable descriptive form. A **good** Situation will describe the business domain clearly and put the problem in context. An **excellent** Situation will in addition to providing context, be objective to the point of being pedantic.

In order to describe the business domain clearly, it is necessary to have to a substantial level of detail, and there are words that are clear indications that the level of detail is insufficient. '**Need**' is one of those words. I've found it is common to see among first drafts from my product managers something along the lines of "…the doctor **needs** to know all patients that […meet some criteria or other]." This statement is begging to be decomposed. **Why** does the doctor need that information? Is it that doctors actually need the information for itself, or is that information just one way in which the final result (filing a regulatory report, saving patients' life) is achieved? Drilling down into such broad generalized statements will get us to the detail that is important to provide accurate context.

Detail is important, but equally so is objectivity. We should guard against sweeping statements or emotive phrases. Using emotion is a subtle and unwelcome way of introducing implicit assumptions, and these are dangerous to a business case. Beware of value-laden terms. Compare the effect of "1,000 patients **die**…" versus the value-laden "1,000 patients **perish**…", or even "1,000 patients die **needlessly**…" which is also a value statement and a generalization substituting for detail. Remove the word "needlessly", and replace it with facts illustrating why it is needless, for example "… 1,000 patients die **from a disease curable for $10**". Who knows what having the additional information that it costs $10 to cure this disease might have on the eventual solution?

Other words on my watch-list include vague comparatives such as '**More than** 1,000 patients die'. '**About**' conveys the roughly the same information without setting off emotional alarms. "It is *critical* that…" and other leading phrases can also be eliminated, either because they are redundant or because they can be replaced with the supporting facts. Stripping out implicit assumptions and emotional responses is important because the Situation is the foundation upon which the rest of the business case will be built. If the Situation is contaminated with overly broad statements, exaggerations, or misstatements it will weaken the credibility of the business case and, even more seriously, may even affect the solution that is delivered to market. The Situation is normally the longest section of the SPIN.

Problem

The Problem section is intended for capturing issues with the current situation. If *detail* and *objectivity* are the bywords for the Situation statement, then *perspective* is the byword for the Problem statement. Urgency is one such perspective to be particularly wary of. Sometimes I see product managers define problems as if there was no alternative and the end of the world was imminent. It is very rarely the case that there is not a workaround to any given problem. If there is a workaround in place, then the problem isn't that the task can't be done at all; it is that the workaround isn't complete in some way. A well-defined problem statement will focus on what that gap is. For example, in the case of a report the problem is rarely that the information can't be found without the report being generated from the system, but that manual compilation is tedious and inaccurate.

This example also illustrates the danger of *solutions in disguise* discussed above. "The problem is that doctors can't […run a report from the system]" isn't a problem; it's specifying a solution ("create a system report"). The Problem section may run to half a dozen bullet points or so, but should be reasonably succinct because the Situation should have made clear the rationale behind the problems being highlighted in the first place.

Implication

The Implication is the reason why the problem is costly in some way to the user. Implications generally fall into four distinct categories: time, cost, quality, and usability. Because Key Performance Indicators (KPI) are derived from implications, the Implication section is important. It will form an enduring thread throughout the Agile governance process.

If the Situation and Problem have been well specified, the implications will be relatively obvious, and if the implications have been well captured, it will be easy to wrap quantitative KPIs around them. Implications are typically three to five bullet points. I like to group them by category (time, costs, quality, and usability). The Implication should be solely from the customer's perspective. A statement like, "the implication is that we are losing sales to competitors" has no place here. Save that for the business justification part of the template. Believe me, your customers don't care one bit that you are losing sales!

Needs

For the Needs statement, I prefer to express the needs as **structured** connextra similar to the familiar user story connextra. Needs are not requirements in the sense of functional or non-functional system requirements, but area more akin to abstract market needs. The purpose is to communicate specifically why the need exists and whether it is to make a **decision**, or to perform an **action**.

"Decision Needs" are indicated with verbs such as 'determine', 'identify', 'assess'. The generic pattern of the Decision Need connextra is "… [to obtain some sort of information] *so that they can*… [make some sort of decision]." "Action Needs" on the other hand, use verbs such as 'update', 'add', 'change', 'report', 'investigate'. The generic pattern of the Action Need connextra is "… [to do some sort of action] *so that they can*…[achieve a result or outcome]". The result or outcome will use words like 'report to', 'audit', 'save time', 'reduce cost', 'determine'. The skill in writing both types of Needs is to express it in such a way that the scope boundaries are clear enough to the business analyst without specifying the actual solution. Needs connextra should be *specific* and *descriptive*.

- **Specific.** If it is too vague, then the product managers have absolved themselves from making a decision. This situation often manifests itself in over-generalized outcomes. For example: *"the nurse needs vitals information in order to save lives"* rather than the preferred *"the nurse needs vitals information to determine whether to alert a doctor."*
- **Descriptive.** If it is too prescriptive it pre-empts the business analysis. For example: *"the nurse needs an email"* rather than the preferred *"the nurse needs to be alerted."*

Both "decision" and "action" Need connextra begin by indicating the *primary actor*, the *priority*, and the *implication category*. The pattern for the beginning of the connextra is "[Somebody] [has a level of urgency] [to address implication of]…" Some examples of this pattern include:

- Analysts must have an easier way to…[time/cost/usability]
- Nurses should have quicker way to…[time]
- Doctors must have safer way to…[quality]
- Accountants should have a more accurate way to…[quality]
- Firemen could have a cheaper way to…[cost]
- Teachers must have a clearer way to…[quality/usability]

Putting this all together:

Generic Form of the Need Connextra

[Somebody] [has a level of urgency] [to address implication of]...

...[obtain some sort of information] *so that they can*...[make some sort of decision]

OR ... [do some sort of action] *so that they can*...[achieve a result or outcome]

Example of a Need Connextra

"Pharmacists should have a quicker way to find patients undergoing antimicrobial therapy with normal or trending downward temperature so that they can decide whether to make changes in the drug regimen."

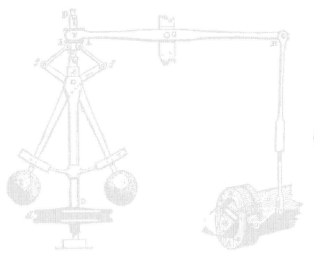

IV. Agile Governance Templates

Introduction

Both project gates and portfolio reviews depend on documentation. Earlier we discussed the role of Agile governance in documenting the known information, the prevailing assumptions and the current plan. We highlighted the role of such documentation in provide transparency, capturing assumptions, demonstrating 'due diligence', providing a 'baseline' for the project, and overall, facilitating clear thinking. We will be looking more closely at the documents that help us do this. They are:

- **The Market Strategy**. A three to five year strategic plan driven by macro factors.
- **The Annual Plan**. The annual budget and product roadmap, with milestones.
- **The Delivery Plan**. Detail of the milestone - at the "last responsible moment".
- **The Project Closure**. An objective report on the success of the milestone.

I prefer rich standardized templates with lots of sections in them. I use these documents to capture the expectations and assumptions that were current at the time the document was written. I also use templates to help all value stream participants to think logically, and as 'best practice' checklists.

There are several objections that as a PMO I hear when, to their utter dismay, I inform someone that they need to fill out a template in order to get approval through the governance process. These objections come from both management and the Agile software development teams. Let's see if we can understand where these objections come from and examine appropriate responses. We'll look at four different objections that are often heard from management and from the teams:

1. We don't need documentation because we all know and agree what the situation is, so writing it down is just a waste of time, so we are not going to do it.
2. It will take far too long to write down all the information required in the template so we not going to do it.

3. Documentation is not Agile, so we're not going to do it.

4. We don't know the answer to all the questions being posed in the templates, so we can't do it.

OBJECTIONS FROM MANAGEMENT

1. We Don't Need Documentation Because We All Know and Agree

I sometimes encounter resistance to documentation because at the time it is considered to be unnecessary. Documentation is a tool against waste – the waste of starting down one path only to have that path arbitrarily reversed. Even, or perhaps especially, if it seems obvious to all concerned, writing down the current state of knowledge avoids ambiguity in the future. There are two reasons for making sure this gets down in writing. The first reason is that everyone will be making different assumptions – of that I can absolutely guarantee. The second is that even if there was 100% agreement on what those assumptions are today, in three or six months or two years' time when we are evaluating the project again, no one will remember what their assumptions were at the time - so best to get them written down now!

When an assumption is subsequently proved wrong, or new information is made available, or the market has changed, then having the prevailing assumptions written down will make changing the plan easy and transparent. I can't tell you the number of times this has proved true for me. Many months after a decision has been made, someone invariably starts questioning its wisdom, asking for the business case or user analysis or whatever. Of course, by then it is too late to create it.

2. It Will Take Too Long To Write Down All The Information

Either the appropriate amount of research has been done and completing the template is easy, or the appropriate level of deep thinking has not been done and completing the template is hard. Even if the research has been done and it should be easy, the template itself can cause pause. When breaking in a new product manager I will often get a call complaining how impossibly long the template is, and how they couldn't possibly complete it – they are far too busy, and they would like to tell me why it is not necessary anyway.

For me the interesting thing about this phone call is that it frequently lasts as long as it would take to actually complete the template. As an Agile PMO I am never too busy to do someone else's work for them (at least the first time) and will end up taking dictation, filling in the template for the product manager on this call. However, because I occasionally take editorial liberties when I do this, the product manager soon learns that they are actually not too busy to make sure that in future their business case reflects their prejudices, and not mine!

OBJECTIONS FROM AGILE TEAMS

3. Documentation Is Not Agile

The Agile manifesto stresses individuals and interactions over processes, and working software over documentation. Unfortunately in many governance situations, individuals, interactions and working software just aren't sufficient. There are many characteristics of the larger product development value stream that make it quite unlike the software engineering process. To consider a few of the differences between the Agile development environment and the rest of the value stream:

- **Agile methodologies encourage collocation** (for example in a single large room) for development teams. In theory we could squeeze the entire value stream participants into a room, CEO and all, but it is not recommended!
- **Agile encourages blended non-specialist teams**. In theory we could create a blended product marketing/management/user research team for the upstream value stream process, but these tend to be specialist, non-interdependent roles so in practice this is unlikely to happen for organizations of any size.

- **Agile methodologies encourage discrete batches of work** that are processed serially, minimizing overall lead and cycle times, where an ideal cycle time is a single iteration of 1-4 weeks. The value stream is a much longer-running process with cycle times of up to 1-3 years. Remembering detailed information for that length of time just isn't practical!

4. We Don't Know The Answer!

Software development teams are frequently consulted during the early stages of the value stream to get their inputs on possible technical solutions and estimates. However, teams are used to working primarily at the later stages of the process where their estimates are quickly translated into commitments that they are then held accountable for. Asking team members to estimate a project that is only in the early stages of planning, and is therefore barely defined, can be a difficult and unfair situation to put the team in. We should remind ourselves and the teams that we are not looking for facts, but for best guesses based on assumptions. What are those assumptions? What is our level of confidence in those assumptions? Remember that in Agile governance the assumptions are the plan. As those assumptions are proved true or false the plan will be modified and updated. However, we need a starting point and best guesses are as good a place as any. The principle of pooled variability teaches us that even bad estimates, when summed together in aggregate, can be surprisingly accurate. As long as our estimates are 'unbiased' (as equally likely to be too high or too low), then when we aggregate them the errors cancel each other out.

In summary, templates and documentation are needed as part of Agile governance, and they are entirely consistent with Agile principles. They are needed:

1. To facilitate responding to change
2. To manage alignment and hand-offs
3. To create transparency

The Market Strategy

A market strategy is a plan for your product that looks out as far as three or five years, and possibly even longer depending on what sort of business you are working in. It is perfectly legitimate to ask ourselves what is particularly Agile about developing a three-year plan – after all surely Agile is about moving away from 'big up-front design'? Creating a long-term plan appears incongruous in the context of small batch sizes and making decisions at the last responsible moment. We know there will be a lot of waste generated by attempting to look that far ahead, and the degree of uncertainty will be extremely large, making the plan almost worthless. So why would we try and plan out three or more years in the future?

It takes time to create great software. A consideration with Agile that is often overlooked is that in order to develop a prioritized, valuable backlog, a lot of work has to be done beforehand. The value stream starts with knowing *what* market problems you are solving. However, before we can know what market problems we are solving we have to determine what 'the market' is, and then have to find some problems that need solving. We don't need to have much detail, but we should have a reasonable set of testable hypotheses of both those things or it doesn't matter how good the rest of our Agile process is – we will have already failed. As organizations go from competent to good to excellent in their Lean/Agile adoption we would hope to see that such long lead times become much shorter, but for now a three year strategic horizon is I think realistic for most enterprise software systems.

The Agile governance process expects a market strategy that is focused on the market problem. We are looking for a market strategy that does not have much solution design. If we see solutions at this stage it may indicate that sloppy thinking is occurring, because problems are a lot harder to analyze than solutions are to dream up! So what is a market problem? Pragmatic Marketing™ defines a market problem that is worthy of consideration as being one that is:

1. Required to be solved in a timely manner (*urgent*)
2. Experienced by many customers (*pervasive*)
3. One that customers are willing to pay to have solved (*valuable*)

Even if formal Pragmatic Marketing™ hasn't been adopted at the organization these three criteria are excellent ones for any Agile PMO to build into a decision framework. 'Urgent', 'Pervasive', 'Valuable' align very well with the 'customer' focus that Agile also evangelizes, and these three together ensure that the organization is focused on addressing important and valuable customer needs.

The market strategy provides essential context to the business and market problems. Rich context is therefore an important goal of Agile governance, and while this is true throughout the process, it is particularly important for the documentation of market strategy. Having this context enables collaborative interactions to occur as we move through the value stream. It is also through context that the *intent* of strategy is best communicated.

MARKET STRATEGY PORTFOLIO REVIEWS

Market strategy is the most important thing a company does. There is no point in building a better heffalump trap if there aren't any heffalumps. If it is serving the market strategy properly, the Agile governance process will be managing upside "*opportunity*" rather than downside "*risk*". In order to effectively manage opportunity we should do so by way of means of a multi-step executive-led approval process.

The executive approval process needs to be multi-step because good market intelligence is generally scarce and expensive. A multi-step process allows us to iterate and elaborate on the opportunities, so that as the field is gradually whittled down we will have more time to spend on the details of the best opportunities. We want to provide just enough information to allow a decision to be made on whether to stop pursing the opportunity or continue to the next level of elaboration.

A MARKET STRATEGY TEMPLATE

Category	Types of Information to Provide
Market Definition	Market Segments
	Buyer & User Personas
Competitive Landscape	Competitor Threats
	How to Win / When to Run Matrix
	Alternative Solutions
Financial Analysis	Market Sizing
	Pricing
	Revenue Projection
	Product Profitability
	Key Performance Indicators
Go To Market Strategy	Positioning
	Barriers to Buy
	Distribution Strategy
	Launch Considerations

The Market Strategy Template Explained

1. **Market Definition**: "Who is our target?" Definition of the market segments, the buyers, and end users that exist within that market.

2. **Competitive Landscape**: "Who do we need to beat?" What is the backdrop to the competitive strategy? Consider both direct and indirect competitors and identify the competitive strategy for each – are you expected to compete head-on to displace am incumbent, or will you attempt a differentiation strategy for example?

3. **Financial Analysis**: "What is it worth?" Market sizing, pricing strategy, and high-level revenue projection and product profitability estimation is useful to be included in this section. Information at this point will be scarce and inaccurate, so order of magnitude estimations and capturing the assumptions behind those

estimates should be the focus. This section is important, however, because it signals to each stage in the value stream the size of the scope and consequently how much effort is expected to be expended on the project.

4. **Go To Market Strategy**: "How will it be sold?" How the competitive strategy will be executed. Market positioning, the distribution strategy and other launch considerations.

ARCHITECTURAL AND INTERNALLY DRIVEN PROJECTS

Technical projects such as architectural re-engineering, and operational efficiency and/or quality improvement projects follow a template. Although still part of the same product development value-stream, they represent a variation to the process, while still being perfectly consistent with the Agile governance framework. The exact nature of the templates and documentation required depends very much on what those projects are, and the business environment. As such they are out of scope of this book, but nevertheless the basic principles of staying focused on the problem rather than the solution hold true, and all projects, whether market-driven, technology-driven, or operation-driven should be evaluated in the context of the overall strategic goals of the organization.

The Annual Plan

I have found that the term 'roadmap' is one of the more ambiguous terms in Product Management. I mean it here to refer to a medium term (6-18 months) plan of major features that we intend to deliver to market. In the Agile governance process, I would expect the roadmap to be revisited at the very minimum each annual planning cycle, and perhaps as often as once a quarter. In this section, therefore, I will assume that the roadmap is part of the annual project planning cycle, and that its review is congruent with the budgeting cycle.

The annual plan is the "handoff" document between product marketers and product managers. Product Management is being given the mandate to plan and develop the roadmap, along the path set by Product Marketing. The annual planning document is an input into the decision-making process, making the case for "why this" and "why now". It also should capture the purpose, or intent, of the initiative. The market problem is described, along with additional information such as market intelligence, proposed milestones, context within the long term strategy, and high-level technical input including technical design, estimation and resource planning. Milestones are a collection of one or more related features, constituting the high-level phases of the development plan, and will be the granularity (in other words, the batch size) of further analysis in the delivery plan documents.

AN ANNUAL PLAN TEMPLATE

Category	Types of Information to Provide
Market Problem Definition	Market Needs
	Context & Use Cases
	Problems to Solve
	Customer Impact
Market Intelligence	Buyer Analysis
	Competitive Landscape
	Market Evidence, Industry Presentations & Conferences
	Regulations and Best Practices
	Direct Customer Feedback
	Customer Support/ Feature Requests
	Win/Loss Analysis
Solution Analysis	Technical Analysis
	Current Capabilities Gap
	Dependencies
	Alternative Solutions
Go to Market Strategy	Launch Strategy
	Sales Strategy
Business Justification	Business Objectives
	Strategic Alignment
	Key Performance Indicators
	Financial Analysis
	Cost of delay Analysis
Roadmap & Project Plan	Product Roadmap
	Business Milestones
	Resource & Cost Analysis
	Assumptions, Risks, Constraints

The Annual Plan Template Explained

1. **Executive Summary**: "What do I need to know?" Short summaries on why the market cares, why the Business cares, and the bottom-line costs and resource implications that will give a context to a casual reader. Write this section last and make it truly a summary of the detail in the main body of the document.

2. Market Problem Definition: "What is the problem?" Extracted from the market strategy, elaborate on only those specific aspects of the overall market problem that is intended to be addressed in this (12 month) period. Provide rich background context, specify the problem, and describe the expected customer impact. These can be further illustrated with use cases.

3. **Market Intelligence**: "How do we know?" This section is an encapsulation of all the research and market knowledge that has been gained in order to reach the decision to proceed with this particular market problem. Just as the market problem definition is derived from the problem statement in the market strategy document, the market intelligence will be too. Summarized evidence from the market, regulatory constraints, and customer feedback should all be included.

4. **Solution Analysis**: "What are we building?" High-level technical analysis from the architects and business analysts addressing questions such as the technical capabilities gap, the build/buy decision, and alternative solutions to be considered. Detailed solution design is neither necessary nor desired.

5. **Go to Market Strategy**: "How will it be sold?" Will this be a stealth release pushed to existing customers, or an all-out market launch of a new product? Detailed plans are not required at this time, but for each of the milestones to be delivered this year there should be some consideration given to the Marketing and Sales departments' calendars.

6. **Business Justification**: "Why should we care?" From the perspective of the Business, not the customer. It includes budget, completion / success key performance indicators, and the cost of delay. Concentrating on only the features being planned for this year, the details in this section are high-level - giving just

enough information that competing annual plans for different initiatives can be compared and contrasted during strategy planning.

7. **Milestones & Project Plan**: "How are we doing it?" If the project is to be delivered in several stages then each stage is a milestone on the roadmap. Any resourcing constraints, assumptions, and risks are highlighted in this section, but Do not attempt a detailed work breakdown schedule or other phased planning approach, for obvious reasons.

ARCHITECTURAL AND INTERNALLY DRIVEN PROJECTS

Technology-driven and operations-driven projects should be considered alongside market-driven projects during annual planning. The business justification should be based on the analysis of cost savings, scaling and supportability considerations, among other non-functional requirements. The standard template should be modified accordingly. The Scaled Agile Framework (Leffingwell, 2011) suggests that annual budgeting is done through top-down allocation of resources, and I also have found this to be a reasonable and natural approach to planning. I have also found that it is often harder to execute in practice than it sounds!

The Delivery Plan

The delivery plan is the actual plan for the backlog that will be given to the solution development teams to execute. Further elaboration of the annual plan will be required because the annual plan is too high level and fuzzy to be implemented directly. This elaboration will be of the milestones on the roadmap. Whether or not milestones are independently releasable, they should be the atomic governance artifacts and therefore each one should have its own delivery plan. Because milestones represent the batch-size within Agile governance, they should be as small as possible, while being big enough to satisfy at least the "minimum viable product" criteria, if not the "minimum marketable product".

Release Planning versus Milestone Planning

An early version of Agile governance that I implemented was to solve the problem of too many decisions being made. A root cause we identified was that the product manager didn't really know what the roadmap should be, and was therefore being highly reactive to sales and one-off customer demands. A Quarterly release plan was the counter-measure we instigated. Product Manager was required to create a gate document with estimated stories for the upcoming Quarter. This counter-measure worked as intended for about two years -the teams were able to execute a multi-year initiative, and to do so one Quarter at a time. The business domain was highly complex and so the planning for the next Quarter of work itself took a Quarter to create the requirements for, however. This long lead time led to huge backlogs of work (after two years, we had built up a backlog of two-years worth of stories in the 'new' queue. This was obviously mostly waste, as we were never going to it. Wasted work and long lead and cycle times have led me to now recommend that instead of planning whole releases, we should plan, in strict serial order, one milestone or feature at a time, never getting too far ahead of the teams.

DELIVERY PLAN PROJECT GATES

In complex systems where some design upfront is necessary I have found that two project gates are generally appropriate for development approval. The first gate sits at the boundary between Product Management and the solutioning teams/UX/architects, while the second sits between the solutioning teams/UX/architects and development. This sounds rather Waterfall. It isn't because these milestones are small – they should not be more than one month's work from start to finish, and the gate documents themselves are written at a high level.

In larger systems these two gates will define the entry and exit phases of the user experience, architectural and interaction design. In smaller Scrum processes only the first gate may be required, merely serving to approve the milestone onto the backlog for development.

1. The first gate is a 'design' gate, and indicates that the milestone has business value and should proceed to design.
2. The second gate is a 'development' gate, and indicates that the design approach is considered adequate and so we can proceed into the Agile software development process. In small systems this will happen inside the sprint or during sprint reviews.

Whether or not your Agile governance process has one or both of these gates will depend largely on the complexity of what is being built, and therefore understanding how and why each of the gates is important will enable you, as an Agile PMO, to determine whether you need them or not in your process. Let's discuss each of these gates in detail.

The First Project Gate

I suggest that the first gate should be owned by the product manager, and be viewed as the hand-off document between the product manager and the downstream solution design team comprising of business analysts, architects, and user experience designers. Before this then, we will have created an annual plan that will have a fair amount of background information on the problem, the financial business case, and a high level roadmap. However not much, if any, work will have been done on defining the actual backlog within the milestone. Getting to this backlog will take some considerable effort, and so this first gate is required for approval for that effort to begin.

The gate is weighted heavily towards business justification and problem analysis and will reference the annual plan heavily. However, unless your annual plan only has one milestone, this new gate document will go beyond the annual plan, elaborating and focusing on only what this one milestone will achieve. For example, the business justification will not just be a repeat of the justification made in the annual plan, but will be specific to this one milestone. It will describe the business benefit of this deliverable in and by itself – as if the other milestones on the roadmap that were referenced in the annual plan do not exist. Indeed they may *never* exist if business priorities change in the future and the roadmap is changed!

The benefits might well also be quite different from those stated in the annual plan, especially if this is the first deliverable on the roadmap. The deliverable for a first milestone is likely to be a market or technical proof of concept, or it might be mostly foundational work with only marginal immediate commercial value. In both of these cases the purpose of the deliverable would be markedly different from that captured in the annual plan for the whole, multi-phased project. The value and purpose of this specific deliverable should be carefully and diligently captured, because this will have an important impact on the downstream Agile processes in helping define the backlog priority. It will also be important in helping to defining 'adequate' or 'fit-for-use' during the launch decision for the milestone.

The Second Project Gate

Once the first gate has passed approval the design team can get to work in earnest. *Now* is that "last responsible moment" to complete the majority of the user research and architectural design that we've been waiting for. The output of this phase is the fully estimated and prioritized backlog of stories. At the very least it will comprise of descriptions of what the 'customer' value proposition is. I prefer to have the business analysts or user research team "own" the second gate document and be accountable for it.

This implies making the researchers accountable for analyzing the use cases correctly and for properly prioritizing the user stories. The researchers and designers - and not the product manager - should be accountable because if the product manager is to be accountable for the actual story minutiae then they are being asked to understand both the use cases and the solution design in depth. If that is the case you probably don't need your business analysts because the product manager will be doing their job anyway! Whichever way you manage roles and responsibilities, the second gate is when the solution design, the estimates, and the schedule, are finally approved by the Business. After this gate, the Agile teams are let loose to design, code, test and deploy the solution.

A DELIVERY PLAN TEMPLATE

Category	Types of Information to Provide
Executive Overview	Proposed Solution(s)
	Business Justification
	Project Constraints
Market Problem	Context
	Problems to Solve
	Customer Impact
	User Research
Business Objectives	Key Performance Indicators
	Financial Analysis
Project Management	Go-To-Market Strategy
	Project Scope
	Risks
	Assumptions
	Constraints
	Key Roles and Responsibilities

The Delivery Plan Template Explained

1. **Executive Overview**: "What do I need to know?" Each proposed feature should be documented with a brief description of the solution, the problem being addressed, and the benefit that is expected to the customer. Capture the budget allocated to this milestone, and the value proposition for the Business. Highlight the most significant and uncertain assumptions.

2. **Market Problem**: "Why are we doing it?" It is important to ensure that the market problem is as tightly defined as reasonable because the delivered solution will be directly measured against how well it solves the problem. Use cases are often an easy, understandable way to communicate this. Also include the expected customer impact/benefit and list the justifying user research.

3. **Business Objectives**: "Why do we care?" Even though the scope of the project might not be completed, it is perfectly possible that many, if not all, the business objectives will be met, therefore the enumeration of the business objectives is perhaps the most important part of the entire governance process. The success or failure of the project will be measured against these objectives in the future.

4. **Project Management**: "What are we doing?" A list of prioritized features, the go-to-market strategy and any risks, assumptions and constraints. The list of features is almost an afterthought in this document, despite the fact that by this time a considerable amount of work would have been spent on solution design.

ARCHITECTURAL AND INTERNALLY DRIVEN PROJECTS

At the time of solution design there should be little difference between projects that are internal or externally generated. An advantage of operational or technical projects over market-driven ones is that the 'customers' are much more readily available to the team. For internal projects we can invite the actual end users to be an active part of the design process, and this process can be very empowering and rewarding for all involved, especially if the lead times are extremely short with development following immediately after designs have been finalized with the end users.

The Project Closure

We are required to capture the project costs so that the Accounting department will be able to expense or capitalize the effort appropriately – however this is not the *primary* purpose of producing formal project closure. Within Agile governance the purpose of closure is to capture as succinctly as possible what *has* been done, what has *not* been done, and what is *still to do*. The Agile "change management" process does not track the path of how the project has arrived at its final state, nor does it provide any formal way to capture the final project result. As a consequence of these deliberate omissions the Agile governance process must fill in these gaps. We make an exception to the Agile Manifesto by creating this documentation because the primary consumers will be stakeholders in the future with whom collaboration is not possible.

The last version of the delivery plan that passed through an executive approval gate is used as the baseline. This baseline delivery plan will be used to compare the difference between what was actually achieved and the original intention. The emphasis should not be on whether this or that requirement or feature was delivered as planned, but on *whether the project results or outcomes were achieved as intended*. This is a somewhat subtle but extremely important distinction.

Results and Summary Explained

1. **Project Purpose**: "Why did we do this?" A direct copy from the delivery plan is sufficient, outlining the customer benefits and the business justification.
2. **Realized Outcomes**: "What value has been gained?" If they were specified in the delivery plan, the KPI for project completion and KSI for project success should be revisited in light of the completed scope and current market information. This

A PROJECT CLOSURE TEMPLATE

Category	Types of Information to Provide
Results and Summary	Project Purpose
	Realized Outcomes
	Project Variances
	Project Statistics
	Lessons Learned
	Next Steps
Feature by Feature Progress Analysis	Market and Business implications of the scope that was completed
	Consequences of the incomplete scope
	Recommendations for next steps
Project Variance Analysis (for major changes in scope or budget)	Issue
	Response / mitigation
	Financial Impact
	Schedule impact

is where we should declare victory or defeat for the project. Often a project ending in defeat provides more information than one that is declared a success. We treat failures as welcome and necessary parts of the feedback loop!

3. **Project Variances**: "Which assumptions were wrong?" A tabulation of variances, totaling up the budget and schedule impact to provide reconciliation with the original budget. This transparency is an important part of the feedback loop. It demonstrates that the project team understands the business realities of the project, which in a healthy organization will lead to mutual trust between the project teams and the rest of the organization, and especially with the executive team.

4. **Project Statistics**: "What are the facts?" Information required for accounting such as hours worked or total cost. A tabulation of features and their

completion-to-plan status. Any Agile statistics that the organization tracks from project to project such as velocity.

5. **Lessons Learned**: "What should we do differently?" Conclusions from retrospectives that are relevant to the overall project and governance, but excluding purely technical and team learnings. Executive and management input is highly desirable in this section, as are any suggestions of how we can improve the Agile governance process itself.

6. **Next Steps**: "What should we do now?" Make a note of any upcoming roadmap items that are related to this one. Recommendations for new follow on projects and any other changes to strategy.

Feature-By-Feature Progress Analysis Explained

By the time a project finishes, the project team will have been working through the backlog and will have been handling project changes sprint by sprint and story by story. The state of the card walls will reflect the final state of the project at the moment the project ends. However, the card wall is ephemeral and so we should try to capture its information as soon as possible. Using the card wall we extract the state of completed and not completed stories and group them by priority. If multiple market problems, use cases, or features were addressed during the release, then the analysis should be first subdivided to reflect each one separately. In and of itself, the listing or tabulation of the individual stories is not useful. The stories do, however, provide a starting point for the product owner to review the scope that was completed. Referring back to the assertions made in the baseline delivery plan, the product owner should be able to answer three questions for each use case or feature:

1. What are the customer and business benefits of the scope that was completed? This is a description of which benefits are expected to be achievable given the scope that was completed. They may or may not align completely with the base-lined anticipated benefits.

2. What are the customer and business consequences of the scope that was **not** completed? If a few low-priority stories were missed, the consequences might be minor usability conveniences, but on the other hand if important stories were missed, there may be hoped-for business outcomes that are now no longer achievable.

3. What are the recommendations for next steps? Does the product manager and/or product owner feel that the feature should be considered 'done' based on the implications and consequences of the complete and incomplete stories, or can the Business expect future work requests for this feature? Should the marketing or sales plans for this feature be adjusted?

Project Variance Analysis Explained

Agile handles minor changes to the features and stories themselves as part of the Agile framework. Major changes in project scope or assumptions are captured separately - somewhere in the Agile governance framework at the time that the changes occur, or very soon after. Formal escalations and notifications of major project changes are in keeping with the goal of transparency and accountability that the entire value stream should be striving for. We ask the product or program manager to document these events as they happen and to escalate them to the executives and other stakeholders as necessary. Apart from a description of the issue and the change decision, the information to be captured is the impact to the project from a budget, schedule, market, and business perspective. In the closure document it is sufficient to either append the individual project variance reports, or to summarize them.

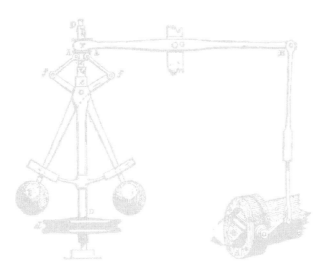

Conclusion

Succeeding With Agile Governance

In section I: "Problems of Governance" we discussed three problems that are often seen in organizations adopting Agile, which work against Agile principles. Defining features too early in the process will prevent the elaborative benefits of Agile to be properly leveraged. Making too many decisions at the wrong times will prevent the benefits of Agile cadences from being properly leveraged. Requiring Waterfall artifacts will prevent the waste-reduction benefits of Agile from being properly leveraged.

In section II: "Agile Governance" we discussed how cadences should be used to reduce waste when switching priorities. By investigating the need for perpetual planning throughout the value-stream we uncovered two fundamental properties of Agile governance:

1. Agile governance is more concerned with the *planning* than it is with the plans themselves. When we plan, we formulate hypotheses based on certain assumptions. If we capture those assumptions in the governance process we can test our hypotheses in the market and know which assumptions are being tested. We capture assumptions so that as contradictory facts emerge we know which assumptions to change and which plans need to be modified.

2. Agile governance is more concerned with *problem definition* than solution design. It is during the Agile software development process that solutions are designed, not in the upstream governance processes. We have come to understand that the real business value comes from identifying market problems that are urgent, pervasive, and that someone is willing to pay for in order to solve. Therefore the focus of Agile governance is on the problems themselves, and not the features or requirements to solve those problems.

In Section III: "Agile Governance Techniques" we outlined some practical tools to help with the demands of perpetual planning, how to use project gates and portfolio reviews for demand management, ways to focus on the problem space using SPIN, and how to use the Cost of Delay to plan projects and metrics to evaluate projects. Finally, in section IV: "Agile Governance Templates" we presented four template outlines that provide transparent and meaningful context for problems and interpretration of project results. Together these four outlines cover the full governance value stream from the market strategy, to the annual plan, the delivery plan, and finally to the project closure.

I am not claiming that "succeeding with Agile governance" is a final destination. In this book I have not attempted to lay out an ideal theoretical Agile governance structure. Agile governance supports an Agile development process. It is not necessary that Agile governance is itself "Agile", or that it is perfectly optimal with respect to product development flow. It is my belief that at the time of writing in 2014 there just is not enough understanding of what such a theoretical "Agile Governance" structure would be, nor how a perfectly Agile organization, with perfect flow, would look like or behave. Instead, and until that time arrives, in this book I have attempted to provide practical ways to modify current governance practices in order to make them compatible with existing Agile software methodologies. It is my hope that you will take some value from my experiences, apply these and other teachings to your own problems as they become apparent to you, and continually develop your own understanding of what makes an organization Agile. Good luck!

I invented Agile...and SO CAN YOU!"

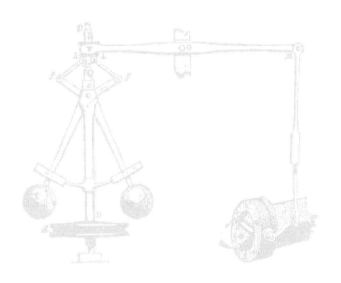

Appendix

The Agile Manifesto

No Agile book should be without the Agile Manifesto (Beck, et al., 2001) displayed prominently. I am a signatory to the Manifesto because the Manifesto is a source of inspiration and guidance to me.

We are uncovering better ways of developing software by doing it and helping others do it. Through this work we have come to value:

Individuals and interactions *over* processes and tools
Working software *over* comprehensive documentation
Customer collaboration *over* contract negotiation
Responding to change *over* following a plan

That is, while there is value in the items on the right, we value the items on the left more

Kent Beck, Mike Beedle, Arie van Bennekum, Alistair Cockburn, Ward Cunningham, Martin Fowler, James Grenning, Jim Highsmith, Andrew Hunt, Ron Jeffries, Jon Kern, Brian Marick, Robert C. Martin, Steve Mellor, Ken Schwaber, Jeff Sutherland, Dave Thomas

© 2001, the above authors
This declaration may be freely copied in any form,
but only in its entirety through this notice

The Muda Manifesto

I created the Muda Manifesto several years ago out of my frustration with Lean's 'Seven Sources of Waste'. I know that the Toyota Production System lists seven types of waste that are very applicable to manufacturing but I sometimes have trouble in relating those wastes to service organizations. Those seven wastes are motion, overproduction, conveyance, inventory, unnecessary processing, waiting, and correction of defects.

After some thought about what caused waste in a software development organization, I came up with the **Muda Manifesto** - 'muda' from the Japanese word for 'waste'. The Muda Manifesto is designed to be broadly applicable to most situations.

The simplest thing that works *over* exhaustive solutions
Failing fast and iterating *over* making it perfect the first time
Creative problem solving *over* rigid processes and procedures
Collaboration and team work *over* specialization and hand-offs
Self-organization and empowerment *over* dependence on supervision

That is, while there is value in the items on the right,
we value the items on the left more

Works Cited

Beck, K., Beedle, M., Bennekum, A. v., Cockburn, A., Cunningham, W., Fowler, M., et al. (2001). Retrieved from Agile Manifesto: www.agilemanifesto.org

Cohn, M. (2006). *Agile Estimating and Planning.* Upper Saddle River, NJ, 07458: Pearson Education Inc.

Cooper, R., Edgett, S., & Kleinschmidt, E. (2002). *Portfolio Management: Fundamental for New Product Success.* Reference Paper, Stage Gate International.

DeMarco, T., & Lister, T. (2003). *Waltzing With Bears: Managing Risk on Software Projects.* New York, NY, 10027: Dorset House Publishing Co, Inc.

Drucker, P. (1986). *Innovation and Entrepreneurship.* New York, NY, USA: HarperCollins Publishers, Inc.

DSDM Consortium. (2012). *Agile Project Management Handbook* (1.1 ed.). Kent, United Kingdom: APMG-International.

Leffingwell, D. (2011). *Agile Software Requirements.* USA: Pearson Education, Inc.

Rackham, N. (1988). *SPIN Selling* (1st Edition ed.). USA: McGraw-Hill, Inc.

Reinertsen, D. (2009). *The Principles of Product Development Flow.* Redondo Beach, CA, 90277: Celeritas Publishing.

Sixtensson, A. (2012, 2 20). *Lean Magazine.* (Softhouse) Retrieved 1 6, 2014, from Cost of Delay – interview with Don Reinertsen: http://leanmagazine.net/lean/cost-of-delay-don-reinertsen/

Sliger, M., & Broderick, S. (2008). *The Spftware Project Manager's Bridge to Agility* (1st Edition ed.). (A. Cockburn, & J. Highsmith, Eds.) Boston, MA, USA: Pearson Eduction, Inc.

The Balanced Scorecard Institute. (n.d.). *The Balanced Scorecard Institute*. Retrieved 12 14, 2013, from Balanced Scorecard: www.balancedscorecard.org

Made in the USA
San Bernardino, CA
22 February 2014